To my sweet si[st]er Kris.
I found this [...]
of fun + insp[i...]
It reminded m[...]
Enjoy the read –
Love,
Martha

courage to be
YOU

courage to be
YOU

Inspiring Lessons from
an Unexpected Journey

Gail Miller

with
Jason F. Wright

**DESERET
BOOK**

SALT LAKE CITY, UTAH

Library of Congress Cataloging-in-Publication Data

Names: Miller, Gail, 1943– author. | Wright, Jason F., author.
Title: Courage to be you : inspiring lessons from an unexpected journey / Gail Miller with Jason Wright.
Description: Salt Lake City, Utah : Deseret book, [2018] | Includes bibliographical references.
Identifiers: LCCN 2017051444 | ISBN 9781629724270 (hardbound : alk. paper)
Subjects: LCSH: Miller, Gail, 1943– | Mormons—Conduct of life. | Mormon women—Biography. | Businesswomen—Utah—Biography.
Classification: LCC BX8695.M545 A3 2018 | DDC 289.3092 [B] —dc23
LC record available at https://lccn.loc.gov/2017051444

Printed in the United States of America
LSC Communications, Crawfordsville, IN

10   9   8   7   6   5   4   3   2

To my mother, Myrtle O. Saxton,
who taught me what real courage is.

"Courage is the most important of all virtues,
because without it we can't practice
any other virtue with consistency."
—MAYA ANGELOU

Contents

CONTENTS

Acknowledgments

As I think about those who were instrumental in making this book a reality, I am reminded of a quote by Melody Beattie that says: "Gratitude unlocks the fullness of life. It turns what we have into enough, and more. It turns denial into acceptance, chaos to order, confusion to clarity. It can turn a meal into a feast, a house into a home, a stranger into a friend. Gratitude makes sense of our past, brings peace for today and creates a vision for tomorrow."

I feel gratitude to the people who have helped me see the value in my life and encouraged me to share what I have learned with others. I am humbled that my experiences seem to have more than one purpose. I have grown in unexpected ways, been enriched beyond my capacity to contain, learned abundant lessons with each trial, and felt the hand of the Lord in every step I have taken. These things make what I have enough and more.

Because I feel deep gratitude for those who have given me

help along the way, I would like to specifically acknowledge a number of very special people.

To Lynn Scoresby, a close friend and guide through many of my difficult times, who planted the first seed that a book about my experiences could be beneficial to other women who might be experiencing the same things, I say with deep sincerity, thank you!

To my son Bryan, who persisted when I doubted, who set up a schedule of interviews when I would have put it off, and who encouraged me with words like, "You have *lots* of things to say that will be interesting to others." I hope he is right. Thank you, Bryan.

A special thank you to Andrew Johnson for his kindness, his gentle encouragement, and his willingness to take on this project—to ask questions and record interviews each week until we had the beginnings of a manuscript.

Thank you to Jack Sanford, who filmed the interviews and never made me feel like a blubbering idiot when I cried during the emotional stories.

Robert Bell and Carisa Miller were also helpful in the interview process. Thank you for your encouragement!

I will be forever grateful to Jason Wright for his extraordinary ability to extract stories of general interest from our interviews and for convincing me that others might benefit from my experiences. He has a beautiful gift for writing. I could not and would not have written this book without his guidance, encouragement, and expertise. Jason, you are exceptional.

I must also recognize the enormous efforts of Deseret Book, specifically Sheri Dew, Laurel Christensen Day, Lisa Roper, and Emily Watts. It's been an honor to work with them.

I want to acknowledge my husband Larry, who passed away in 2009, our children, Greg, Roger, Stephen, Karen, Bryan, and Zane, their spouses, and our posterity for the major role they have played in my journey through life. The older I get, the more I know I don't know—they have been my willing teachers.

To my husband Kim, a quiet, gentle man with an unmatched patience who loves me just the way I am: Thank you from the bottom of my heart!

My acknowledgments would not be complete without my including all the other people who have contributed to my life: friends, coworkers, employees, neighbors, church congregations, my parents, my siblings, and my extended family. Each of them has enriched my life. They have generated untold rewards, challenged me in ways that have made me stretch beyond where I thought possible, and, in the end, helped me to create a beautiful quilt from that fabric called "life." I have been richly blessed.

A Letter from Gail

Dear Friend,

When I was a young mother balancing the endless demands of five children with their school lessons and sports, my own Church assignments, and a nonstop husband, the idea of writing a book never entered into my consciousness. I was so consumed with living life that I had no time left to write about it. As the years passed, I began to feel a need to record my life's journey. In reality, I couldn't imagine anyone being interested. Honestly, sometimes I wondered if my own family would read it.

But . . . here I am.

It seems I've traveled a million miles from those days dominated by ball games, never-ending loads of laundry, parent-teacher conferences, and Church callings. I'm an empty nester now, and I have no problem confessing how much I miss those times. If you're caught in the middle of that whirlwind, I promise, someday you'll miss it too.

Today, as I look back over my life, I recognize I have been blessed with a wide range of experiences: some simple, some complex, some ordinary, some extraordinary. I've experienced everything from being a timid, unsure housewife and stay-at-home mom to being the owner of one of the 200 largest privately owned businesses in the United States. I'm confident my experiences haven't been better or worse than anyone else's, but they are uniquely mine and they make up the fabric of my life.

Looking through that lens, I clearly see that one of the most beneficial qualities I've embraced is courage. I've had the courage to look inward and face my weaknesses and challenge my trials. I've also had the courage to look outward and welcome the future. I have been blessed to use my courage to grow and expand my God-given talents and potential when the opportunity was before me. I've worked hard to create a life of purpose, direction, and satisfaction.

I'm grateful for all the experiences, good or bad, that have been placed in my path and have allowed me to exercise the courage to uncover God's plan for me.

I hope as you read about my journey, you will recognize a gem or two of truth that may be useful in your journey. Hopefully, you'll recognize you're not alone in a confusing and complicated world. Maybe you will have an "aha moment" when something I've been through gives you the courage to face the hard things you're going through.

Courage is like a muscle—the more you use it, the stronger it gets. May you have the courage you desire to become the best "you" possible.

Sincerely,
Gail

Have a Little Faith

Finding It and Keeping It

When my son Greg was five years old, he approached me in the kitchen with his typical curiosity and asked, "Mommy, where does God live?" He had no idea how the question would change our lives. Without that question, I'm not sure I'd be writing a book, and certainly not one with a chapter on faith.

It was the early 1970s, and my husband, Larry, and I were still adjusting to our new life in Colorado. He'd become unhappy with his job in Salt Lake City at a small car dealership, and when an opportunity to play competitive softball in a new city came along, Larry and I discussed it and decided it was something we should explore. Just like that, he landed a job at a Toyota dealership in Denver. We'd been in our own home in Salt Lake for only eighteen months, but this was an opportunity we couldn't pass up. As for me, I was excited for the chance to be a full-time mother to our two boys and another baby on the way.

When we left Utah, Larry and I hadn't been active in the faith of our childhood—The Church of Jesus Christ of Latter-day Saints—and we didn't exactly advertise our Church membership when we arrived in our new community. Back then it wasn't hard to hide when you moved from one area to another.

I love that memory from more than forty years ago, because Greg couldn't have known that when I was five years old, my own parents were sharing stories from a set of children's books packed with Old and New Testament favorites. When I was a child we didn't have traditional family home evenings or a regular schedule of family prayer, but I knew where God lived. I was very familiar with Jesus Christ, Noah, and Moses, and I loved hearing their stories come to life. My upbringing wasn't perfect, but Mom and Dad were doing their best, and that foundation of faith had deep roots.

I had stayed active in the Church in my late teens during the awkward transition from Young Women to Relief

> WHEN I WAS A CHILD WE DIDN'T HAVE TRADITIONAL FAMILY HOME EVENINGS OR A REGULAR SCHEDULE OF FAMILY PRAYER, BUT I KNEW WHERE GOD LIVED.

Society, but soon after that, my involvement dropped off for a while. It wasn't that I'd forgotten everything I'd learned; I think I just forgot what the Spirit felt like and how it spoke to me. I was working, supporting my parents' family, and dating Larry as if it were a full-time occupation.

People I meet are sometimes surprised to hear that Larry and I both faded from the Church for a time. Certainly I never doubted that the faith of my ancestors was true and that Christ's gospel had been restored in the latter days. But there was a disconnect between *believing* and *living* like I believed.

With young Greg still looking on and his question hanging in the air, I knew it was time to stop hiding. I had to go back to church. I immediately hunted for the phone book and began calling local chapel phone numbers. Eventually, I found the ward we lived in and learned that Primary met on Wednesday afternoons. It took courage I didn't know I had, but I took the kids that very week, and everyone was eager to invite me to Sunday meetings, too. I will never forget the Primary president embracing and loving my kids as if they'd always been there. We weren't treated as *lost,* we were treated as *found.*

I don't remember the name of every brother or sister who has been a blessing to our family through the years. But I clearly remember Bishop David Brown and how he visited sooner than I expected, and one of his first questions still rings in my ears: "May I send home teachers?"

My husband said they were welcome, but he was too busy to sit in. Larry Hunter and Steve Carpenter were assigned to our family, and these must have been the two most dedicated men in the ward because they never gave up. They didn't push, but they found ways to fellowship with kindness and genuine interest. At first my Larry remained upstairs; then he slowly gravitated to the kitchen, still out of sight but well within earshot.

I kept praying for Larry to have the same change of heart that I was experiencing, but he wasn't ready yet. He was softening and growing supportive, but he kept getting more and more entrenched in work and softball. Before long, I was attending Relief Society, Sunday School, and sacrament meeting and taking the children by myself. It was a challenge to keep them all quiet and interested, but I did my best. Since we had to pass one on the way home, sometimes I would bribe them with a trip to McDonald's if they behaved. It was a choice I probably wouldn't make today, but it's something I will never regret. I believe that when you're doing all you can to rekindle the family's faith, the Lord is willing to look past the Golden Arches and into your heart.

After what seemed like an eternity, Larry finally attended

a Relief Society social with me and met many of the members of our ward. He didn't change his mind overnight, but our wonderful home teachers were making inroads by their sheer consistency. I was praying like I never had for him, and I realized that the prayers weren't just about him. They were about me. Despite his disinterest in returning, I was learning to love him more than ever. I knew I couldn't personally will him back to church. Maybe more than anything, I realized I wasn't so much praying for his mighty change of heart as I was praying for mine and hoping he would take notice.

No praise of home teachers is complete without an equal dose, maybe more, for visiting teachers. Inspired Relief Society presidencies have always assigned to me exactly the right sisters for what I've needed. During this time of my returning to the Church, a phenomenal visiting teacher came every single month with a list of what was happening in the ward and stake. Even though I wasn't always there for those events, I was connected. It's intriguing that something as simple as a ward calendar can make someone feel loved.

When our bishop was released and called as stake president, I felt uneasy and worried that Larry's progress, and maybe mine, would slow to a crawl. Instead, the new bishop didn't miss a single step. Bishop Lowell Madsen loved Larry as if they'd known each other forever. Though Larry was still less-active by every measure, he was asked to accept a calling as an assistant volleyball coach. Larry agreed, and the call soon grew to head coach.

I remember once telling Bishop Madsen how well Larry was doing in his new career. "Tell him he'll do even better if he comes to church!" The exclamation was strong, inspiring, and true. How the Lord loves a courageous, loving leader!

HOW THE LORD LOVES

A COURAGEOUS,

LOVING LEADER!

When the priests quorum adviser moved out of the ward, Bishop Madsen called Larry back into his office. Was he willing to join the bishop in working with the priests on Sunday? Always on his toes, Larry explained that he had commitments to play softball on Sundays during the summer. "How many Sundays do you play ball?" the bishop asked.

Larry backed into the equation. "There are fifty-two Sundays in a year. I play from May through September, which takes about twenty Sundays and leaves about thirty-two Sundays free."

The bishop smiled. "I'll take them." It might have been the first time in the history of the restored Church that the terms of a calling were negotiated like a business deal! It's humorous, but that experience taught me so much about how we view those who don't fit the mold. That certainly described our family well.

It was such a new experience to have Larry go to church with us. The boys in the quorum loved him and he loved them. It was also time for Larry to buy some new scriptures and really study the gospel. He always loved working with the youth, and near the end of his life he said that it was his favorite calling—the best calling in the Church.

A year later, Bishop Madsen called Larry in and told him it was time for him to receive the Melchizedek Priesthood and to be ordained an elder. Larry wasn't sure this was something he was ready for, but he wanted to listen to the questions for the Melchizedek Priesthood interview without answering them so he would know exactly what would be expected. The bishop went through the interview questions one by one, and Larry listened intently, but he didn't answer. They agreed that he should go home and think about it.

Once again, things went more slowly than I'd hoped. Larry was deliberate and methodical. He kept teaching the young men in priesthood meeting, studying the scriptures, and working very long hours.

Finally, one morning while Larry was at work, the bishop called him on his private line to ask him to come in for another interview. This time he wanted him to answer the questions. They were both very busy men and, remarkably, the only time they could find to meet was 10:30 p.m. When Larry got to Bishop Madsen's home, the bishop told him that he'd had a dream the night before about Larry that was so vivid, he'd gotten up in the middle of the night to write himself a note to call the next day. What the bishop hadn't known is that that very morning, Larry had said to me as he walked out the door for work, "Gail, I have put this off long enough. I need to call the bishop today."

As they went through the questions again, Larry answered candidly. He told the bishop that there were only two issues that concerned him. "I have a problem with swearing," he admitted. Larry added that he only swore around men, but he promised to work on controlling it. The second was more serious: "I don't pay tithing."

The bishop asked why, and I've always imagined that Larry's simple reply must have caught him off guard. "I don't know. I just never have." The bishop invited him to begin paying immediately and promised things would change if he did. Late that night, when Larry returned, he told me he was ready to be ordained and that I was to start paying tithing without fail. "Pay it on my whole check on the next payday and never ask me about it again." He did not want to be tempted to change his mind.

The next payday was January 5, 1979. I paid the tithing and hoped that things would start to get better for us. Larry was looking for peace of mind about work, and I was looking for him to be more involved with the family.

Our lives changed forever over the next few months. On a vacation to Utah, Larry had lunch with the owner of the dealership where he'd once worked. By the end of the lunch, they had an agreement written on a napkin. By the end of the day, they had a formal agreement, and Larry wasn't just working for a dealership anymore. He owned one.

We weren't naive about the source of the opportunity or the tremendous blessings that were soon to come. We believed that returning to church, paying our tithing, and doing our best in our callings had resulted in the Lord opening the windows of heaven. Our family was sealed one year later in the Salt Lake Temple.

No one who was in the sealing room that day will ever forget some very specific counsel offered by the sealer. Remember that we owned just one dealership, Larry didn't do his own advertising, and he wasn't any more recognizable to the general public than I was. Still, the sealer looked at us both and said that he felt strongly impressed to tell us that Larry's name would be known by thousands, even tens of thousands in the years to come. We were dumbstruck. We couldn't imagine ever getting to a place where that many people would know us. Larry H. Miller was a man, not a brand.

One might think this is where our fairy tale begins. From the day we strolled out of the temple, surrounded by Utah and Colorado friends, including those loyal home teachers who helped get us there, everything should have unfolded perfectly. We were living the commandments the best we could, we had been through the temple, and our children were being raised in righteousness. At last, we were ready to rest our spiritual feet and coast.

Hardly. Over the years that followed, we learned the same lessons that many families learn. Just because we draw closer to the Lord, the trials don't end. Just because the kids are sitting in church, they haven't lost their agency.

> JUST BECAUSE WE DRAW CLOSER TO THE LORD, THE TRIALS DON'T END.

We tried to hold family home evening, but Larry's schedule made it impossible to do anything traditional. I tried alone, but I wasn't very successful. When Larry made time to join us, he felt he needed to make up for lost time, and we would spend an entire evening, even up to four hours, trying to have the perfect family night. If there's one bit of advice I'd hope to pass along to another family, it's this: Don't try that at home.

I convinced Larry we needed another approach, and it might not look like what we saw in the Church magazines. We'd pick him up at work and spend a few minutes together or go to his ball games. Sometimes we'd go to a movie or dinner and then take him back to work. Monday nights weren't usually spiritual, but, as often as possible, we did things as a family.

Though rearing our kids wasn't what I'd envisioned, I made a commitment to teach the basics. We learned to forgive, to be compassionate, to not carry undue burdens, to listen, and to talk. We weren't always in the same room when we experienced the lessons, but Larry and I learned that the Lord's beautiful gift of agency wasn't just ours. Our kids had it too. Through trial-and-error parenting, we accepted that the kids didn't have to be just like us. They got to choose who they'd be, both inside church and out. As they grew and spread their wings, as most kids do, we constantly reminded them that we wished they would come to church and they were always welcome, no matter how many weeks or months had passed.

I don't know who first said it, but I love this quote and

still put it to use as often as I can: "They don't care how much you know until they know how much you care." Being a Christian means loving people, pure and simple. More than checking any boxes, I wanted my family to know that sincere love was always the answer.

I now have five children, thirty-five grandchildren, and fourteen great-grandchildren. By the time you read this, that last number is bound to be higher! Some are active in the Church, some aren't. Nevertheless, they all know that to me, there's nothing like the gospel. But they also know there are other ways to live a good life that are connected to gospel principles. Really, isn't that the very definition of a good life? It's impossible to strive for goodness and not be living some gospel principles, whether a person is in a pew on Sunday or not.

I can't recall when it started, but when the kids started marrying and having children of their own, we decided we would host a multigenerational family home evening once a month. We meet on a Sunday night, and the door is always open to any and all, no questions asked. Whether they're active in our faith, some other religion, or none at all, we continue to teach what we know to be true. Anything else wouldn't be true to who we are.

Some of my grandkids are open about having very

different viewpoints on life and religion. When these topics come up—and we encourage that—I remind them that the foundation of our family is stronger than our opinions. I want them to feel loved and accepted in my home no matter what they believe, where they worship, or whom they date. The Savior would never lock a door on us, so we shouldn't lock Him out of our lives either.

During my growth in the gospel, I developed talents and an ability to look at problems, evaluate them, ask if there were a better way, and then find it. I learned the core of that trait from my mother.

THE FOUNDATION OF OUR FAMILY IS STRONGER THAN OUR OPINIONS.

At church I once found myself explaining to a mother how to make a soldier hat out of an oatmeal box for a Primary program. I was brand-new in the ward and didn't know her or her abilities very well. She listened very intently and said "thank you" when I was finished with my impromptu lesson. I told her I would come and help her anytime she needed more assistance. She sweetly said she'd call me if she got into trouble.

When the day came for the big program, her child's was the best-looking and best-constructed hat, bar none. After the program, someone mentioned who the mystery woman was. I was embarrassed and humbled. That woman was President Ezra Taft Benson's daughter and a very dedicated mother. Being a prophet's daughter didn't make her any more special than you and me, but she had plenty of experience and had made many more costumes than I had. Still, she saw an opportunity to listen, be polite, and forgive my arrogance. I learned a real lesson that day: I needed to be more humble and not so overbearing. That lesson would come in handy many times.

After serving in the Church as a secretary or counselor on several occasions, I was called as a Relief Society president. Trust me, I would've been perfectly content to never serve in this calling, but I've also come to understand that the Lord had specific lessons in store for me. I remember when the calling was extended, Larry told me, "Gail, you have supported me for a long, long time, and now it's my turn to support you." I admit I was worried that my service might take away from him, but he was true to his word and supported me in every way.

I was conflicted. I felt inadequate from day one. I didn't truly know if I had the courage to take on a responsibility that could dwarf me. On the other hand, I knew I'd lived an un-expected journey and might have experiences and lessons that could be valuable to women I worshipped with. Alongside my counselors, I had some sacred experiences ministering to sisters. What a blessing it was to remind them that no matter what they were living through, the Lord was keenly aware of them. I hoped that when I was released I wouldn't be remembered for fancy dinners or visiting teaching statistics, but for spreading the Lord's love every chance I had.

I also witnessed how everyone is at a different place in his or her life, and we need to allow that. We have to accept that some people will know more than we do, others will know less, and God doesn't want His sons and daughters trying to wedge into someone else's place. We need to find our own. The best way we can do that is by staying faithful, by being ourselves, and by saying "yes" to callings that scare us.

I think that's one of the reasons The Church of Jesus Christ of Latter-day Saints is so beautiful. It gives us the platform to do all the things we need to do in this life. It gives us opportunities to teach, to speak, to learn, to share, to

> GOD DOESN'T WANT HIS SONS AND DAUGHTERS TRYING TO WEDGE INTO SOMEONE ELSE'S PLACE. WE NEED TO FIND OUR OWN.

serve, and to love. It gives us everything we need to live life fully, if we avail ourselves of it. That's the key: taking advantage of it all, but not falling into the trap that you have to do it all at once.

Recently a friend asked me what was the most unusual trial I faced during my time serving as Relief Society president. The answer is easy. One of our ward members lost his home in a fire—twice! His name was Kim Wilson, and a few years after their fires, his wife passed away from complications of a very long illness. Larry and I knew the couple well, and sometime after Larry died, Kim began an old-fashioned courtship. I resisted initially; I had no intention of remarrying. But once again the Lord knew best, and I said "yes" to a second marriage and the promise of righteous companionship.

Kim is an accomplished attorney in Salt Lake City and has been tremendously successful in his own right. But he is unlike Larry in many other ways. Not better, just different. Kim was a bishop at age twenty-eight, he's been in five bishoprics, he served a mission, and he's probably never missed a Sunday church service. Also, we live in a different ward now. (I'm in charge of the smoke detectors.)

Kim drives our morning and evening prayers, but I have to do some nudging on scripture study. Every night I get out my iPhone, and we follow along in bed as the voice on the LDS Gospel Library app reads us the Book of Mormon. Once again, my spiritual routines don't necessarily look like something you'd see in the *Ensign* or a video on the Church website. But for us, it works. Every day that we get to know Christ better is a good day, no matter how it happens, and we shouldn't let anyone convince us otherwise.

When I first agreed to write this book, I didn't know exactly what I wanted to say or how I wanted to say it. I only knew that I didn't want it to be full of heavy-handed advice or trite invitations. However, on the topic of faith, an invitation is exactly what I feel inspired to put on paper.

If you've let the flame of your faith go out, or perhaps dim just a bit, please consider opening up that figurative phone book. If you've forgotten why you used to love the scriptures, open them up again. Make a goal. Read a verse or two.

If you've become less fluent in the language of the Spirit, spend a few minutes on your knees and humbly ask Father in Heaven for a reminder. I promise He already knows the sound of your voice, and you'll soon recognize His.

If you've made mistakes (and who hasn't?), share them with the Lord and one of His ordained bishops. You'll find your bishop to be an imperfect man with flaws like the rest of us, but what he does have is a deep desire to minister and to represent the Lord in the healing process of the Atonement.

If you've lost all faith and you're back at the very beginning of your journey, you might even start with a simple, childlike question. Something like, "Where does God live?"

Marriage and Motherhood

Happiness Is Optional, Mistakes Are Not

I was in the seventh grade when I met Larry. Just after school started in the fall of 1957, he called to say a mutual friend had told him I was cute and we should be introduced. We arranged to meet at my locker the next morning, and though I was a little late, there he stood waiting for me. I remember that the bell rang before we had much of a chance to talk, and I must not have made a very good impression because it was two years before anything meaningful transpired.

In the meantime, we did have a few classes together, including art, and he was the good-looking model for one of our assignments. I could tell he was full of energy and always the life of the party. Sometimes I would go into the gym after school to watch him play ball, and he often did the same for me. We were both athletic and competitive.

Then, as I was walking down the hall one day after school in the ninth grade, I spotted him coming toward me all alone. I walked right up to him and said the words that changed the course of our lives: "Kiss me, Larry." Talk about unexpected courage!

"Okay!" he said. "Let's go into Mr. Hughes's room."

We kissed, and evidently it was a hit, because after we said good-bye, he came by later that day. It was January 30, 1959, and we went sleigh riding that evening on "Bunker Hill," just down the street from my house. We had a great time, and my unexpected journey took a new turn.

We were hardly apart during our dating years. We relished the time together; Larry always wanted me right by his side. If he were working on a car, he loved for me to be right next to him, handing him wrenches or listening to his stories. It was comforting for him. Back then I didn't really understand how much Larry welcomed the feeling of being loved and appreciated. More than once he told me that when he was young, he would lie down by the dryer because it was warm and comforting and the sound of it made him feel good. His parents weren't the sort who hugged him, kissed him, or said, "I love you."

High school was an adventure for Larry. At various times he was thrown out of classes and even his own home. Although his IQ was off the charts, his grades never reflected that. Amid the turmoil and emotional ups and downs, I became the calming influence for him. Despite our struggles in years to come, I was always the emotional anchor in his life.

Six years after that sledding date, Larry and I were married. I knew I was making a "forever decision"—the most important decision of my life. Our marriage wasn't perfect, but on the surface it appeared we had everything. We were frugal, we eventually ran a successful company, our kids were healthy and active, we gave back to the community. But if you've read *Driven,* the book Larry wrote with Doug Robinson, you know that Larry's drive to provide and succeed was extraordinary. And, quite often, Larry gave his best at work and there wasn't much left for the family when he got home late at night.

When I revisit life with Larry from that first kiss to our last, I can't help but think of the role communication played in our marriage. I'm an advocate for a no-secrets approach from the very beginning. I've counseled engaged couples to talk about everything before the wedding. It's crucial to discuss friends, in-laws, parenting approaches, intimacy, money, career goals, and so much more.

Marriage isn't just about love and a white picket fence.

It's a partnership, and no partnership of any kind has ever succeeded without communication. When I think of my married friends who have happy, thriving marriages, it's because they've treated that partnership as the most important thing in life. On the other hand, friends who've dealt with divorce often point to a lack of communication as the poison that killed the marriage. Those are generalities, I know, and sometimes divorce *is* the best thing. But without honest, candid communication, it can become the first resort rather than the last.

> MARRIAGE IS A PARTNERSHIP, AND NO PARTNERSHIP OF ANY KIND HAS EVER SUCCEEDED WITHOUT COMMUNICATION.

I don't know its source, but there is a popular story about a woman getting impatient with her husband because he never did what she asked. She used the trash as an example. The wife would walk into the kitchen and announce, "The garbage smells horrible." In her mind, she was asking her husband to take it out to the garbage can. When that didn't happen, she would become upset and fire away: "You never do *anything* for me. I asked you to take the trash out."

"No," he answered. "You didn't ask me to take the trash outside, you just said it smelled bad."

Over and over in my marriage I learned the value of communication. One of Larry's favorite pastimes after work, particularly later in our marriage, was to soak in our yellow bathtub and download his day to me. I sat next to the tub on the floor and we talked about everything that was happening in the business. Larry had many flaws, like we all do, but he included me in every aspect of his professional life.

We counseled about buying the Jazz, building the arena, building and buying dealerships, leaping into the movie theatre business. He treated me as an equal partner in the company because I was one. I appreciated that whenever he spoke or was interviewed about his success, he always acknowledged me and said it couldn't have happened without my partnership.

I appreciated those moments of talking together, and I loved when he was vulnerable. I don't believe you can really be loved without being vulnerable. You have to truly open yourself up in order for the other person to get to know you enough to love you. When we present only what we want someone to see, that's not true love. It could be attraction, affection, or a connection, but it's not the full package.

Based on what you now know, I'm not sure if this next revelation will surprise you or not. The truth is, there were many times when I considered divorce. Larry did too, and I've often said it's fortunate that we never wanted a divorce at the same time. I thought, "This isn't what I expected. A husband working eighty, ninety, a hundred hours a week? A husband who goes weeks without seeing the kids awake because he left before dawn and returned after bedtime?"

In those hard times, I felt that the Lord was watching over me more than ever. I knew that Larry and I had made promises in the temple, and even though my life wasn't what I'd envisioned, divorce in my case would have been selfish. In fact, I think selfishness is the number-one cause of all divorces. For me, divorcing would have meant putting myself first, above even our kids. Plus, Larry wasn't breaking covenants and neither was I.

> I'VE OFTEN SAID IT'S FORTUNATE THAT WE NEVER WANTED A DIVORCE AT THE SAME TIME.

Again, I acknowledge that sometimes divorce is unavoidable, but the costs are high. I imagined a broken family with five little kids being shuttled back and forth, and none of them having a strong relationship with either one of us. With me going one direction and Larry another, I wondered where the kids would fit in. If I were going to reboot my life and put so much effort into that new reality, I thought I might as well make what I already had work. Larry and I had history, devotion, trust. It wasn't easy, but we shared simple faith that if we never gave up, one day it would get better.

———

I know a lot of women who love pregnancy, and I hope no one is offended, but I didn't like being pregnant—not one bit. I heard other women talk about the glow and how they felt so beautiful. I thought, "Are you kidding me?" I felt ugly and just wanted my own body back. With my first baby I recall asking my mother, "Is this what pregnancy feels like? Because I'm not loving it."

Thankfully, when the children came, I felt confident that I was up to the challenge. I knew raising kids would be the toughest thing I'd ever done, but I also knew it would be a huge blessing. I fully appreciated that Larry and I were in a partnership with our Heavenly Father to create and nourish these little ones. It's miraculous that He trusts women so much He gives us the blessing of motherhood. What a sacred responsibility!

Larry and I had five children, a beautiful girl and four handsome boys. Each was unique, a true spiritual individual. I knew from the moment I first held them that each was meant for our family. I believe then and now that God needed them in my arms, in my home, and that since the very beginning, our journey was meant to be spent together as a family.

As the kids came one by one, Larry was becoming increasingly busy with a company that grew faster than we had ever imagined it would. Although Larry was a wonderful provider and probably one of the hardest-working men to ever live, fatherhood didn't come naturally to him. He was an intellectual genius, but his emotional intelligence wasn't as well developed. It was obvious fairly early in our parenting years that I would be wearing two hats more often than I'd thought.

The result was a deliberate reordering of priorities. I learned to focus on things that needed me most, and it wasn't usually the dishes. I kept a clean house, and organization has always been important to me, but there were times when a field trip or spontaneous walk to the park was more important than a chore. If you've ever had to choose between doing housework or spending time with the kids, I hope you've looked down more often than not and said, "Who cares about the floor?"

I LEARNED TO FOCUS ON THINGS THAT NEEDED ME MOST, AND IT WASN'T USUALLY THE DISHES.

It should go without saying that having their father gone so often was hard on the kids. When Larry would talk about being prepared for something, about having a special calling in this life, I knew that meant something having to do with the business and creating security for thousands of families. It was hard not to resent this. I mean, I didn't mind him having a grand purpose outside the home and I was proud of his accomplishments, but I always wished he'd seen a greater purpose at home, too.

Over time I saw that I had a responsibility to help keep my children from having regrets or harboring bitterness. They went through periods of anger about their father's work habits and stern parenting style, and they struggled over not having stronger relationships with him. They saw their friends having healthy relationships with their dads, and I worked very hard to help them see the good their father was doing, even when it wasn't at home. Once again, all I could do was trust that the Lord was keenly aware of me and my efforts to be the best mother and wife I could be.

Once, when I was discussing my parenting journey with a friend, she wondered if I'd ever been tempted to tell heaven that I wasn't experiencing the kind of motherhood I had signed up for. Would I do it all over again? Did I have regrets? The answer to both questions is an unequivocal "no."

I believe both statements, even though seeming contradictions, can be true. First, I have zero regrets. Second, I wouldn't "do it all over again"—not in quite the same way. There certainly are things I would do differently.

If I went back in time, I would marry Larry again a million times. We learned eternal lessons together, and I know my marriage to Kim is better because of them. I'm not afraid to say I still love Larry very much. Death doesn't change that. I know Kim loves his late wife just as much.

To be sure, I would definitely do some things differently with Larry. I would have used our open lines of communication to insist that he participate more with our family each day. I would have asked more forcefully that he develop parenting skills at the same time I was. It wasn't that we didn't want to do it or we weren't willing to do it. It was that we just didn't know *how* to do it. I would have lovingly demanded that we look for more creative ways to solve problems together. Obviously, I would have invited him with more force to do less at work and more with the family and to understand that we both needed to parent equally.

Today, I realize that for all I might do differently, we did pretty well, given the hand we were dealt. My children are all better than Larry and me in every way. When my sons were frustrated, I told them many times that they would have two chances to experience fatherhood—the father they got and the father they want to be. It might sound more harsh than I intend it, but I usually added this: "If you don't like the one you've got, then you become the one you wish you'd had." Without exception, they've all done that, and I know Larry was extremely pleased with the legacy they're leaving as dads, even if he might have regretted portions of his own.

In between the frustrating patches, there were memories made that we clung to in Larry's final days. I'm sure we still do. The experiences taught me how vital it is not to get overly discouraged by what we don't have and to be thankful for what we do. It's a lesson many families can probably appreciate.

One of our favorite activities was four-wheeling in southern Utah. We went as often as we could to Elephant Hill. It's a beautiful boulder configuration, and at certain points the ride gets quite scary. The kids loved it, and I know they admired their fearless dad.

We also went to a place called Shafer Trail. It's a switch-back trail cut in the side of a steep mountain, and you can't see it looking straight on, but when you're on it, it's wild. Larry let the kids ride in the luggage rack on the top of the Land Cruiser. It made me nervous, but they loved every minute.

When Greg was twelve, we decided to take an unusual

family vacation. The Land Cruiser was packed, but we hadn't made any decision on where to go. We pulled out of the garage and stopped at the first intersection at the bottom of the hill. "Okay," Larry said. "Should I turn right or left?"

The kids chose, and at every corner we would ask again and let the kids choose where they wanted to go. Eventually we climbed to the top of Mount Baldy in Utah. I remember it was snowing as we reached the top, and we didn't have jackets. Karen was just four years old and Bryan was a baby, and I carried him the whole way to the top. It's a trip I'd take again in a blink.

On another trip, this time in Colorado, we stopped for gas, a snack, and a bathroom break. I was last in the restroom while everyone else piled in the car. A few miles later, Roger said, "Dad! Aren't you going to wait for Mom?" Thankfully, they turned around.

We didn't always have to leave home to have adventures. We cherished movie night and, as often as possible, gathered for Hallmark movies. Larry and I bought each of the kids a half-gallon of ice cream of whatever flavor he or she wanted. As long as we watched the movie together, they could eat as much or as little as they chose. I can still see them clutching their own cartons and spoons, savoring each spoonful.

When I consider my friends, acquaintances, and business associates, I recognize that some have been married for many years to the same spouse and have wonderful children who've all served missions and been married in the temple. Others are on a second marriage because a spouse was unfaithful or simply left, or because both made mistakes and divorce was the best possible outcome and a chance for a clean start. Others have never been married, or cannot have children, or have lost husbands to accidents or illness. No doubt some have children who earned their Eagle Scout awards or Young Women medallions, served missions, and since have left the Church. I believe no matter the circumstances, the Lord is equally aware of every single one of us. He doesn't withdraw because our lives don't turn out the way we dreamt when we were children. We're not living our vision of our lives anyway; we're living His.

I certainly never planned on raising a grandson, but I did. When my daughter became an unwed mother, I knew in my heart that Larry and I would end up raising the baby. He was a delightful

THE LORD IS EQUALLY AWARE OF EVERY SINGLE ONE OF US. HE DOESN'T WITHDRAW BECAUSE OUR LIVES DON'T TURN OUT THE WAY WE DREAMT WHEN WE WERE CHILDREN.

child, and he gave us another opportunity to be parents. He was twelve years younger than my youngest, and that presented some unique challenges.

More than anything, we wanted him to have a positive experience with the Church. During the years he resisted going, we held the line and told him that as long as he lived with us, church was what the family did on Sunday mornings. Our goal was simple. We wanted him to realize the value of eternal families. We wanted to plant seeds, cultivate them, and wait for them to take root. Like all parents, we hope our children realize who they are, and that one day they'll say, "I want this family forever. And there's only one way to get it."

Our unexpected Act Two of parenting took another turn when this grandson started his education. He had some learning disabilities, and the tough times began early in grade school. We tried private school for a couple of years in junior high, but it wasn't a good fit. It took a lot of pondering and prayer, but I realized his best hope for a good education would be homeschooling. It wasn't easy, but I chose to homeschool him from ninth through twelfth grade, and when we started, I discovered he had never learned his times tables. By the time we finished his senior year, thanks to a mixture of me, BYU Independent Study, and various homeschool websites, my grandson had developed a love for learning and was on his way to mastering algebra. Those years taught me that whether children are in public, private, or a homeschool environment, what they most need is a safe place to learn and for someone to have time to look them in the eye and show they care. I loved raising that boy, and although he still calls me "Mom," he knows I am really his grandmother. He has also maintained a good relationship with his mother. When I reminisce about those times, I think his experience of being raised and educated by his grandmother took much more courage from him than it did from me.

By the time this grandchild came along and hit the standard benchmarks of childhood, Larry was home a bit more and was witness to some of the important moments. He would come to me sometimes with excitement in his voice, "Gail, did you see what the baby just did? Our other kids didn't do that."

I smiled. "Yes, they did. You just weren't there." That was hard for him to hear, but it helped him cherish the memories he still had time to make.

As with Greg, Steve, Bryan, Roger, and Karen, we had to decide at what point to begin giving our grandson freedoms. I always believed there was danger in easing up on kids too early and giving up influence. It can be a tough conversation for parents to have: "When do we make the break between being responsible for them and letting them be on their own?" We never stop helping them up when they fall, but all parents at some point have to stop preventing the falls in the first place. Usually the greatest growth comes when we're willing to let our kids have their own trials.

Mine are all grown now, naturally, but they know that I don't intend to stop giving advice. They can choose to take the advice or not, but a parent's role is to continue to give it. If Heavenly Father never stops giving counsel to His children, we shouldn't either.

Make no mistake, giving counsel is different from keeping the reins on their agency forever. I've always loved something Joseph Smith said: "I teach them correct principles, and they govern themselves." He was speaking of adults, not children, but the concept is the same. At some point, children are mature enough to make decisions based on what they've learned. When children rebel against our advice, as they all will, it might be wise for a loving mother and father to say, "I'm here to raise you, that's my job, and you ought to listen because the time will come when I won't be here. You'll be on your own, and you're going to make big decisions every day. You're learning agency now in my home; one day it will be yours to use fully." In a sense, every parent's goal is to raise great decision makers.

Caution is always wise. As we teach agency and impose righteous limits while our children are in our care, we can't micromanage them. Parents aren't tasked with raising another version of themselves. We can set the standards, but we also need to allow our children to keep their dignity and grow into individuals. There are eternal consequences to raising God's spirit children, and loving parents constantly remind themselves they're raising future mothers, fathers, and leaders in the Church or community. Whatever pathway our children take, the better job we do, the better prepared they're going to be.

I like to think of parenting as a discovery process. We're discovering who our children are and putting them on a pathway that will help get them where they need to go, experiencing both joy and sorrow.

> WE CAN SET THE STANDARDS, BUT WE ALSO NEED TO ALLOW OUR CHILDREN TO KEEP THEIR DIGNITY AND GROW INTO INDIVIDUALS.

I think parents, especially mothers, have a hard time finding that point at which they can let children spread their wings. When do we say, "Okay, this job is yours now. I've done my part. Now it's all yours"? We *always* want to be responsible. We *always* want to take responsibility for our children, for what they do, and either excuse or take the praise. But that's not our job. It's a natural desire, sure, but at some point we must let go and say, "You can do it."

—

Without a doubt, no marriage and family can be healthy without a rich understanding of forgiveness. It's the most important habit a family can develop. The entire plan of happiness, the route back to live with our Father in Heaven, is paved with forgiveness. It's the core of Christ's mission. It should be the core of ours, too.

I've long since forgiven Larry for any shortcomings in our marriage, and I know he's also forgiven me. I know the kids have forgiven us, and they had some sweet times with Larry in his final days that were a balm on the pain of opportunities lost. I think we all recognize that every living person needs forgiveness, just not for the same things.

Many years before she died, my mother began saving every shred of old clothing from me and my siblings. She said one day she was going to make quilts for each of her children. As we grew, the clothes collected in boxes; sometimes I would take something out to remake an item for myself or my siblings, but the quilts remained just a good idea.

When Larry and I moved back to Utah after our time

in Colorado, I finally said to my mother, "Mom, we really should make those quilts. You've been trying to make them all these years. Let's do it."

We picked out the clothes we wanted to use, and I cut out six-inch-square quilt blocks. We laid them out in complementing patterns and sewed many hours together to finish nine quilts—one for each member of the family. As we worked, I'm embarrassed to say there were times I thought, "Why didn't Mom make these quilts when we needed them years ago?" I'm even more embarrassed to say I became a little angry.

My mother didn't work outside the home until she was much older. She had so much time. Why didn't she make those quilts when we were children and our circumstances were so meager? Acknowledging those feelings wasn't my proudest moment, but I learned something pretty valuable. The project, even though it was launched later than I might have liked, made Mom happy. She was a great mother and had done the very best she could within her own circumstances. Isn't that exactly what I've done?

I haven't been a perfect wife or mother either. I'm just doing my very best to build on the legacy of my parents. That's what my mother wanted for me, that I'd be a little bit better than she was. And that's exactly what I want for my own kids.

I want them to sit down when I'm gone and be grateful for what they learned from their dad and me. Then I want them to do it all even better.

I know they will, and I bet yours will too.

The Eternal Value of Hard Work

Teach It; Live It; Reward It

I have such admiration for the life of our elder brother, Jesus Christ. Naturally, there's never been anyone who was more courageous or who worked harder. From the Creation to the Atonement to His influence in every minute of every day of our lives, He was—*and is*—a tireless problem solver, the master of goals, the perfect picture of long-suffering and endurance. Even the most diligent, hardest worker among us will never approach Him in this life, but there is value in trying.

My mother and father were impressive examples of disciples of Christ who worked hard until the day they were laid to rest. From my earliest memory, both worked to provide exactly what we needed, though rarely much more. Our neighborhood earned its name—the Marmalade District—because of the fruit trees the pioneers had planted. The streets all had names of fruit or other things that the pioneers grew: Quince, Apricot, Vine, Almond, and so on. Our home was built in the 1800s by early settlers to the valley, and although it was humble, it had great character. Our yard featured a giant apricot tree that blossomed in early May and bore its fruit in July. Mother always had to have a picture of that tree because it was so beautiful and got better every year.

That special home on Quince Street, where I lived until I married Larry at the age of twenty-one, never had central heating or cooling systems. In the winter, I watched ice form on the inside of my bedroom window. We didn't have extra blankets, so I often slept under old clothes or coats to keep me warm. Usually a new outfit was something Mother had made from an old outfit. We certainly weren't going to the department store to choose new school clothes each fall. Still, this chronic lack of funds created some memorable opportunities for problem solving. Those memories have served me well and certainly will until I'm laid to rest too.

We had one car growing up, and because we did not have money to get it fixed, no one ever drove it but my very careful dad. Having it break down was a risk he couldn't afford to take. When it did break down, he fixed it on his own with improvised tools and parts. I remember watching him more than once make gaskets out of cardboard from a cereal box. He removed the carburetor, brought it inside, boiled it on the stove, and cleaned it. Then he traced and cut a gasket out of cardboard and put the carburetor all back together. Somehow it worked, and if it didn't, he would just do it all over again. I like to think that even if we'd had money then, he would have worked hard to solve these problems on his own anyway.

When our dining-room table was so beaten up it hardly looked like a table anymore, my father bought an inexpensive piece of yellow vinyl, stretched it across the top, and tacked it underneath. It looked so good, and he was proud of it. We all were.

There were days when we turned on the oven and opened the door to keep the kitchen warm. Sometimes we would toast our bread on top of the area heater and wash our clothes in the bathtub. Then we'd hang them on a metal frame or chrome chair set on top of the same heater we used as a toaster. We never bought paper towels or napkins, and sometimes we didn't even have a decent comb. A fork worked just fine to break up the knots in our hair.

When I was in kindergarten, my mother dressed me up as a hobo for Halloween because it was an easy costume to arrange. I didn't realize then how passionate I would become about helping the homeless later in life. It wasn't unusual for me to go to school with holes in my socks and underwear. Motivated to solve that embarrassing problem, I learned to sew my own clothes by the time I was in the fourth grade. A couple of years later I felt confident enough and had enough courage to sew for my friends. I offered this service all through junior high and high school.

My father didn't just teach us to follow Christ's example in solving problems, he also had a knack for creating opportunities for me and my siblings. I was six or seven years old when my dad saw a place selling used furniture. He spotted an old table and a used barber chair and bought them both. I don't remember what he paid, but it couldn't have been much. Back home, he removed the base from the chair and the top from the table, and somehow he attached them together. The base spun rather freely, and he buried the contraption partway in the ground, creating our very own merry-go-round in the backyard. We'd kneel on it with one knee and push off with our other leg to make it go around. If you could get two or three kids surrounding it, they'd push and you could really fly! We played on it for hours. Needless to say, every kid on the block wanted to spend time at our house.

I learned this art of improvisation quickly. When the

straps on my prized roller skates broke, I found some cloth, cut it into strips, and tied the skates to my feet. I was five years old.

Mom played her part too. She cleaned constantly, and I can still picture her almost obsessively scrubbing and scrubbing the outside of a dirty pot until it shone. I'm not sure if that was about cleanliness or about giving her something to focus on besides our hard times. During one particularly lean period, we had very little to eat, and Mother wanted so badly to make bread. She had a little flour, but no yeast. With two pennies in her hand, she walked across the street to the neighborhood store. A yeast cake was three cents, but the storekeeper let her take it on her promise that she'd bring over the other penny in a few days. She was grateful, and she returned home to make the dough. But when she went to put it in the oven, she discovered our gas had been turned off. Humbled but undeterred, she walked to the neighbors' house and asked to use their oven. Fresh bread never tasted so good; it seemed to feed more than it should have.

I never saw my parents take a day off in all my years living at home. For my dad, a shoemaker by trade, a break was a short Sunday afternoon nap. As for Mom, I remember as a young girl thinking, "Does this woman *ever* sleep?" I never saw her slip into bed. She rested upright in a chair, usually

> I NEVER SAW MY PARENTS TAKE A DAY OFF IN ALL MY YEARS LIVING AT HOME.

with a project in her lap. Mom lovingly told us stories that she made up on the fly. On many nights, she was so tired her eyelids would droop and her voice would trail off and she'd say the funniest things that we didn't really understand. "What was that, Mom? Wake up!"

"Where was I?" she would ask before resuming, but it never really mattered. She was such a good storyteller.

Perhaps my most meaningful job as a youth was helping an older woman clean her home. I'd learned much from my mother, of course, but the neighbor who needed me had a much larger home and expensive things to care for. It was a palace compared to my home, and I felt like I was in another world when I walked in.

In her home, she educated me on how to do the kinds of things that preserved the quality of what she owned. I learned how to clean silver and use cleaning tools that we'd never owned in my home. At her side, I had to learn things that I'd never known before. Even though my mother's motto was "Cleanliness is next to godliness," ours was a very humble home.

Soon I realized that my employer had a certain standard, and she enjoyed teaching it to me. I recall cleaning the tracks in the windows where the glass slid. I'd never seen windows like that. We had the old wooden framed windows that were on a pulley. She showed me how to use different cleaners on different surfaces and for all kinds of purposes. In my home, it was soap and water for everything.

Today I see how that experience gave me an important look at how other people do things. I loved the feeling I got when things looked fresh and clean. It was a feeling of accomplishment and comfort. To me, *that's* the real value of hard work. My mother taught me what she could with all the resources she had. This woman did the same, and I was grateful for both experiences.

When I got married and started to build my own little family, the real hard work came from trying to blend two unique people and create a life together. For quite some time after our wedding, I was making more money than Larry was, and our financial security was completely tied up in my paychecks while he spent time trying to find out what he was good at and where he should build a career.

I was going to work, taking care of the household, and

raising children all at the same time. It became my three-legged stool. If I let one leg go, the others would fall. I used to ask myself, What am I doing right now that moves me toward my goals? Like any young mom, I did better on some days than others.

I can honestly say that our years in Colorado taught me more about hard work than I ever wanted to know. I had always appreciated the value of a long day's labor, but Larry was setting a standard with each of his jobs in Colorado that no one had ever seen before, including his family. He worked eighty hours or more weekly and filled his remaining hours with softball because he had a commitment to his team, too.

> I USED TO ASK MYSELF, WHAT AM I DOING RIGHT NOW THAT MOVES ME TOWARD MY GOALS?

Larry used to say, "People ask me how I did what I did." And he would say, "I just went to work every day and did everything I needed to do and then got ready for the next day." So I suppose it hasn't just been hard work, it's been consistent hard work and doing the right things for the right reason. It's a generalization, and perhaps an unfair one, but it's been said that for men, work is someplace they go. For women, work is something we do that begins the moment we open our eyes in the morning. When Larry was away working endless hours, I was trying my best to uphold my end.

On more than one evening, Larry would walk in the front door to see that I still had a lot of things to accomplish. He'd look at me and say, "Why don't you do that stuff during the day?"

Usually I took a deep breath and tried to smile. "I would if I could. I've been working all day too. My workday doesn't just end like yours." Back then, Larry just didn't understand that for women it's never ending, especially when we have children. I was raising kids, keeping a house, caring for the yard, washing the car, all of it.

Eventually I discovered that although I enjoyed working hard, solving problems, and raising my children, I needed some rejuvenation. Sometimes the solution was as simple as saying, "Kids, I need five minutes. Please. No questions. Nothing. Just give me five minutes."

I also discovered that as the family grew, what the children most needed was some one-on-one time. They wanted me to look them in the eyes for a few minutes and just listen. They wanted to be heard. I think I did too.

There were times when I felt guilty about needing that time to myself. But when those feelings crept in, I tried to remind myself that Heavenly Father doesn't build mothers as machines. He created us as human beings, just like our children, with thoughts, feeling, needs, desires, and ambitions.

As part of His perfect pattern, He wants us to learn to work and then teach our families to do the same. But He also wants us to be happy, and happiness comes with balance. I wonder why we forget that we don't just have power to create life, we also have the power to create schedules, balance, and opportunities. We don't have to let our schedule make us; we can and should make our schedule.

As the children and the bank accounts grew, Larry and I made deliberate decisions not to take away the kids' opportunities for work. I saw how some parents wanted to do everything for their children because they wanted them to have what they perceived as a better life. I suppose they hoped for their kids to have the things Mom and Dad didn't have when they were young. But Larry and I wanted our children to feel how satisfying life could be when they worked hard. We thought they needed to experience disappointment and failure as well as success. Of course we helped them when their effort wasn't quite enough to get them across the finish line, but we weren't afraid to let them fail if that was the lesson they needed to learn. We both believed that if they would give their very best, even when they tripped, they were building self-esteem. We looked forward to having them feel the satisfaction of having done something hard.

When our son Greg broke a neighbor's window, we could have hired someone to fix it. But the greater lesson came in assessing the problem, measuring the window, buying the glass, and installing it ourselves. The experience demonstrated that hard work can make up for almost any mistake.

Chores were important to us too. Each of the kids had to clean his or her own room and one more. They could choose which other room they wanted, and the first one to choose got the best choice. We taught them to be responsible, and although ours wasn't always the most organized system, it worked. In today's Facebook and Pinterest world, I wonder if we get more focused on pretty chore charts, rotations, and the perfect plan than we need to. Children just have to understand that working around the house has nothing to do with making Mom and Dad happy, it's about being responsible

IN TODAY'S FACEBOOK AND PINTEREST WORLD, I WONDER IF WE GET MORE FOCUSED ON PRETTY CHORE CHARTS, ROTATIONS, AND THE PERFECT PLAN THAN WE NEED TO.

for the welfare of the entire family. If the family plays together, the family works together.

Work outside the home was also important. Greg was twelve when we bought our first dealership in Utah, and he went right to work as a lot boy. Roger soon started helping in the parts department, and it wasn't long before Steve also worked as a lot boy. Not everyone has those built-in opportunities to provide employment for children. But hard work is never hard to find.

With our diligence paying off, we taught that money also had a purpose. When the kids asked for something, I didn't want to lie to them by saying we didn't have any money. Instead, I said, "We don't have money for that." We needed to be wise and make good decisions with the fruits of our labor. I wish I could say I did this perfectly, and I suspect many mothers are doing it better than I ever did, but I tried.

The idea of society needing to shield our children from disappointment has always perplexed me. Consider sports. Larry wasn't the only athlete in the family; I held my own on the basketball court and softball field. I worked hard for victories and loved getting rewarded, but too often today everyone gets a trophy just for showing up.

Losing isn't such a bad thing. I wanted the kids to learn that failing gives you a chance to work harder next time. If they didn't win today, they could figure out why and give a little more tomorrow. As long as they never give up, I'm perfectly fine with them losing every single time. Winning takes courage, but losing might take even more.

I don't remember when I first heard it, but the analogy of hard work and grades has always resonated with me. When a student works hard to earn A's on his or her report card, we don't demand that the other kids also get A's. It would be ludicrous to say, "You're getting really good grades. What about that boy who's getting D's? Why don't you give him some of your A's so he can pass?" Adults and children alike should be rewarded for what they do and not rewarded for what they don't. The danger of anything less is a sense of entitlement that can spread like a virus.

Today, my testimony of hard work is stronger than ever. I'm still a mom trying to influence my kids—and grandkids—for good. I'm still a wife, now to a second husband, and together we're working to bring our families together as best we can around common interests and beliefs. We're different, to be certain, but we value our diversity and we work hard to see one another the way Christ does.

I'm also still the head of a large company with more than 11,000 employees who rely on a culture of solving problems, creating opportunities, and giving your best no matter where you are on the organizational chart. Of course I'm not doing it alone; I'm surrounded by teams of talented individuals who work hard in their own areas of expertise and aren't keeping score. The important thing is to work hard and make a difference.

President Ronald Reagan had this powerful quote printed on a plaque in the Oval Office: "There is no limit to what a man can do or where he can go if he does not mind who gets the credit." True for presidents; true for the rest of us.

In the area that matters most—conversion to the gospel of Jesus Christ—I like to remind myself that I still have a lot of work to do. I could be wrong, but I think we're never truly converted until we're like the Savior in every way. I suspect even our beloved Church leaders would tell us they have much work left to do, because none of us is ever finished growing, learning, and being tested.

To be clear, I know that none of us can just work our way into heaven. There is no amount of sweeping, dusting, brownie making, or visiting teaching that can secure our place at His side. Only His grace brings us all the way home. But when the time comes, I'd sure like to be found hard at work.

Preferably, doing His.

It's Not about the Money

It's All about the Good It Can Do

One winter evening more than a decade ago, Larry and I climbed into the car for a trip to Provo. At the time, my husband was team teaching an evening class at Brigham Young University. The course was called Entrepreneurial Perspective, and he dearly loved that experience.

Each semester Larry arranged for me to attend one class and teach for him. My lecture was called, "What is it like to be married to an entrepreneur?" The spouses of the students were invited to sit in on this class.

I don't remember how many questions I'd already addressed that night when a brave student raised his hand and asked what perhaps every other person in the auditorium was wondering: "Now that you're in a position to purchase *anything* you want, what would you buy?"

Larry looked at me, and I stood quietly for a moment.

It wasn't that the question surprised *me,* but that I knew the answer might surprise *them.* In that moment—and even now, all these years later—I couldn't think of one thing so important or so exciting that I would rush out to buy it just because I could. So, that was exactly what I said. Larry and I were always on the same page about this: Money doesn't buy happiness and if you have sufficient for your needs, that is enough.

The truth is, I'm not so comfortable writing or speaking about money. Perhaps that's because it's never been important to me. Or maybe it makes me uneasy because I fear there's a tremendous gap between what the public perceives about wealth and the truth.

FOR ME, MONEY HAS NEVER BEEN ABOUT THINGS—IT'S ALWAYS BEEN ABOUT PEOPLE.

For me, money has never been about *things*—it's always been about *people.* And I don't mean which president's portrait is on the front of the bill.

When I was young, a neighbor friend and I conjured up the grandest idea any two girls ever hatched. I was lucky enough to have a huge swing in my backyard that hung by steel chains from a simple but sturdy tube frame. As I learned to do flips while swinging, my friend perfected her balance on the top bar of the frame.

We worked for countless hours on our routine. I remember soaring through the air so high I thought I might fly right around the bar—and right over my friend's head. Then, one day we realized that we weren't just playing anymore; we were practicing for something.

No, we weren't just a couple of crazy girls swinging away after school until our moms called us for dinner, we were a bona fide trapeze act! As I perfected my tricks, she sat or stood on the top bar with her arms stretched out like the star of the Greatest Show on Earth. We were convinced we had something pretty special, and it was time to share it. We went arm-in-arm from house to house inviting every child in the neighborhood to see the show. And what a bargain: admission was just a penny per person!

No one ever offered to take our show on the road, but no one left disappointed, either—and my friend and I learned what it meant to get paid for doing something you love. Today, as I reflect on the memory, I don't see perfect piles of shiny pennies. Instead, I see smiles on the wide-eyed faces of our pint-sized customers.

Now, it's not as if the pennies didn't matter. I was one of eight children crammed into a small house with one bathroom and more needs than resources. When we did have an extra dollar or two, a rarity in those days, we were treated to ice-cream cones for a nickel or a trip to the drive-in movies. There was something special about jamming all of us into a single car and escaping for a couple of hours into a film.

I cherish those memories and what they taught me. Money, clothes, or cars would never bring me joy. I would need *some* money, of course, but all I ever wanted was just enough for my needs. My parents struggled to feed, clothe, and educate us, and I learned quickly that if I needed something, I'd better figure it out on my own. With my mother's help, in particular, I learned how to become a problem solver.

I was born shortly after the end of the Great Depression. Our family was poor. Of course we were—everyone was poor, it seemed. Sometimes we had only one lightbulb in the house and had to move it from room to room so we'd have light in the space where we needed it most.

When money is scarce, food usually is too. My father was a shoemaker and, later in life, a salesman. But it was always difficult for him to make a decent living. With eight children, my mother never worked outside the home. She never even drove a car.

A few years after my friend and I retired our trapeze act, I decided to dabble in the floral industry. I knew how much mothers loved flowers on the table at dinnertime, and I'd discovered the perfect source—a neighbor's yard. Staring at those lilacs was just too tempting, and, without exactly asking permission, I was soon picking bouquets and selling them up and down the street. They fetched a quarter each, and although I loved the coins, the women's joy was even more valuable.

When I was old enough to babysit for some of those same customers, they paid a quarter an hour. In high school I was blessed with the opportunity to clean another neighbor's home, and she paid even more—fifty cents an hour. If I spent a full Saturday on the job, I came home with four dollars.

My only formal job before marrying was at Mountain Bell Telephone Company in Salt Lake City. I was a high school senior and beyond grateful to be employed and have my own money. I loved the work, and I earned up to a hundred dollars a week, which gave me freedom. I decided that, unlike most of my friends who spent carelessly, I was going to save my money for what mattered most. My first sizable purchase was a beautiful bedroom set. For years I'd slept on couches, on floors, and in hallways. I felt so good about working, saving, and then buying that furniture all on my own.

Meanwhile, my mother had been using an old-fashioned clothes washer, and I just knew one day the wringer might yank her finger right off. I worked hard and saved even harder until I could buy Mom her very first automatic washer and dryer with my very own money. She loved it, and I was humbled to help.

Truthfully, I never thought of our family as poor. Instead, I liked to consider all the things I could learn from our meager circumstances. I never went to a church girls camp, bought the latest fashions, or went to the beauty salon. Rather, I learned to sew my own clothes. I cut patterns out of newspaper and made the outfits on a sewing machine I saved for and purchased. When I decided I didn't like the haircuts my mom performed on me anymore, I cut my hair myself. In fact, I cut my own hair for many years, long after money was no longer a driving concern.

When I married Larry, he asked me to cut his hair too. Even years later, when he could have afforded to have his hair cut by the best stylist in the world, I continued cutting it. This was not just to save some money, naturally, but to give us a chance to spend time together.

It was during those first cuts in the early years that we made some important decisions about money. Most important, we pledged that money would never define us and that it would always remain in its proper place. Simply put, money could never become more important than the people earning it.

From day one of our marriage, Larry and I realized that

we needed to be independent, and we promised that we would never go into debt. We didn't want to owe anyone, and we agreed that we'd be happy as long as we had enough money to care for our basic needs.

We remembered this when we first discussed buying a television. It would have been easy to pull out a credit card or finance the purchase through a department store. But we saved for six months to buy a beautiful, twenty-inch, black-and-white RCA TV. Later we bought a kitchen table and chair set that served us perfectly for twenty-five years.

Larry was a hard worker, and he gave everything to find a job that supported our growing family. About five years into our marriage, when we moved to Colorado, we began putting our financial promises to the test. Larry was promoted quickly in a family-owned group of dealerships, and with each position came a healthy pay raise. Though it would have been so easy to use that money to buy this or that and improve our quality of life, we didn't because our needs were already being met.

Just as we'd planned, we began saving or investing every

> WE DIDN'T WANT TO OWE ANYONE, AND WE AGREED THAT WE'D BE HAPPY AS LONG AS WE HAD ENOUGH MONEY TO CARE FOR OUR BASIC NEEDS.

penny. If we didn't need it, we didn't buy it. Then a vacation to Utah changed our lives forever. Larry visited a friend who owned a Toyota dealership and teasingly asked, "When are you going to sell me your store?"

Now, it's important to know this man had politely said "no" many times before. But on that afternoon he simply answered, "How about today?" Because we had agreed on and set priorities, saved carefully, and been unified in our decisions, Larry was ready for the opportunity of a lifetime. And as we continued to work hard, more doors were opened.

However, my family has learned that doors didn't open because of money. Opportunities came along because we tried to live, work, and serve honestly at all times and in all places. We haven't been perfect, far from it, but we've worked very hard to maintain integrity. We've never forgotten that families count on us, and they deserve our best. It might sound like boasting; I'm not shy about saying our shared commitment to families has been evident in everything we've done.

My desire to teach my young family about being frugal began very early. When the sprinkler system failed, I could have called an expensive professional to come and fix it. But why, when I could figure it out on my own? Recently a hand-soap dispenser in my home broke, and the easy solution would have been to drive to the store and buy a new one for a few dollars. No, I don't need a new one, I can fix this and save the money. I committed all those years ago to value what I had, to care for everything as if I could not replace it. Every dollar I don't needlessly spend is a tool that can go somewhere else to bless someone else. I made a point of asking myself, and my kids, for that matter, "Could that money be better used someplace else?"

EVERY DOLLAR I DON'T NEEDLESSLY SPEND IS A TOOL THAT CAN GO SOMEWHERE ELSE TO BLESS SOMEONE ELSE.

As the business grew, Larry became a sought-after mentor. At one point he sat on the board of a large Utah bank. As is common, board members were paid to attend the meetings, and Larry loved collecting a sizable check each time he got to sit with others around a conference room table and talk finance, business strategy, and marketing. But instead of depositing the check into an account, he would cash it on the way home and slide the bills into the pocket of one of his suit coats hanging in the closet.

I knew the routine. That money was there for me to access in a flash anytime someone needed help—no questions asked. Over the years it went to neighbors, Church members, and employees. At the end of the year, we used what was left to help families in need at Christmastime.

As our children grew and took on important roles in the company, those promises Larry and I made were extended to them. Avoid personal debt, treat people with kindness, don't let money rule your lives, and use it wisely. It's better to control your pennies than to have them control you.

Obviously, money gives you freedom, and wanting a little more of it is natural. But having more money in order to accumulate a garage full of toys or a closet so full you can't shut the door can be dangerously addictive. And as quickly as some acquire things, they can be lost.

Since Larry's death, as I have assumed my new role as the head of our family business, I've learned once again that money is still just a tool. It can be either good or evil, uplifting or degrading, and it can enlarge or shrivel your soul. I remember well how many times Larry would ask, "We're not letting money change us, right?"

I told him it wasn't changing who we were, but it *was* becoming a bigger tool for good.

Now and then I think back on those trapeze shows in the backyard of my childhood. I recall that look of satisfaction in the wide eyes of our small audiences. It didn't matter that my friend and I were making money; what lasted was our be-lief that we were doing good with every little talent with which God had blessed us. In fact, sound money management in the twenty-first century is a lot like the parable of the talents two thousand years ago. Are we careful stewards of what we have—growing it, nurturing it, blessing others with it? Or are we squandering it and finding our resources shrinking rather than growing to bless others?

> ARE WE CAREFUL STEWARDS OF WHAT WE HAVE—GROWING IT, NURTURING IT, BLESSING OTHERS WITH IT?

You may have heard in recent years that as chairman of the board and head of the Miller family, I've led my family toward a decision I'm very pleased with. Eventually, all of our wealth, every single penny, will go to a foundation that will give it to worthy causes. Even the crown jewel of the Larry H. Miller Group, the Utah Jazz, has been placed into a trust. This ensures that for decades to come, the team cannot be sold or moved from Utah. I've explained that it's as if someone were putting a billion dollars in the bank and pledging to never withdraw a dollar. The team has been a blessing to our family and community, and we've promised that it always will be.

No matter where any of us are in life, we can make a few simple commitments. Whether we're successful or whether we fail, we must get up again and start over. We don't have to let money change us. We can keep it in perspective. We can bless others with it, even if our means are meager. Larry used to say, "Go about doing good until there is too much good in the world."

There is such joy in independence, and it doesn't depend on bank balances. When we are frugal and take responsibility for ourselves, we will be better prepared when opportunities come our way. And when we're good stewards of whatever we have, we'll find opportunities to help those who can't do for themselves.

I confess that sometimes I wonder what life would be like if we hadn't moved back to Utah from Colorado. Then a flurry of other "What ifs?" will follow.

What if we hadn't bought that first Toyota dealership? What if we hadn't purchased the Jazz? What if Larry had spent all his days running a parts department at a cramped car lot in Sandy, Utah? What if instead of leaving $100 bills in his jacket pockets, he had only been able to slip $5 bills into greasy overalls with the same invitation for me to help a friend in need?

I'm convinced that as long as we're doing good with every penny we have, counseling together often and staying in sync about how to spend, how to save, how to solve problems, and what to teach our kids, we'll have a pretty good life.

Love to Serve—
Serve to Love

Life's Most Inseparable Principles

Though having financial resources has given me opportunities to serve both friends and strangers in creative ways, I've certainly learned that having money is hardly a prerequisite for doing good. Once, when I was a fairly new member of a ward, a sister who had lived for many years in the area befriended me and shared these inspiring words: "The only people I don't love are those I don't know yet."

What a great approach, I thought, and it really opened up my eyes. I needed to meet more sisters! Since then I've seen that while my friend was absolutely right, the motto takes on more meaning with this slight twist: "The only people we don't *love* are those we haven't *served* yet."

When I served as a Relief Society president, I learned

lessons nearly every day about the relationship between love and service and how impossible it is to separate the two. We had one elderly couple I couldn't possibly forget. They were frugal, kind, and maybe just a bit stubborn. But really, who isn't?

The woman suffered from dementia and was a semi-invalid. Her ninety-two-year-old husband cared for her the best he could. He had created his own system and routine and was not aware of the modern conveniences available to make their life more comfortable.

I observed that their nice home was increasingly dusty and the kitchen needed a thorough cleaning. The man was a new chef, after all. It was understandable; his wife's health was failing and he'd made her his priority. It was, however, important for him to get out of the house, so once a week he chose to volunteer at the local hospital. That tells you all you really need to know about his character. Our Relief Society sisters had served them for several years by sitting with her while he was away.

On the days I sat with her, I quickly discovered she needed some additional care. She needed a shower. She needed a haircut. She needed her fingernails trimmed. The kitchen needed to be cleaned. The cover on the couch needed to be laundered. I marshaled all the resources I could, and a small army of women came to help while the husband was away one day. We cleaned the house and took their laundry home to do, and I arranged for some men from the ward to modify the shower and add a grab bar.

The husband was a little embarrassed but grateful for the help. Even with the improvements, though, particularly in the bathroom, he was still at a loss as to how to bathe his wife. So I did what I think anyone else would have done.

I remember how it felt when I stepped into the shower and cleaned her tired, broken body. It was humbling, rewarding, even sacred. She felt like she had value again. It wasn't that her husband didn't love her deeply, but his capacity to serve was limited.

Later that afternoon I cut and curled her hair. I was fortunate to be there when he came home and saw this beautiful, brand-new woman. His eyes shone; they were different. Almost literally, he was taken back to a different time and place with his sweetheart. He was filled with renewed love.

It was an emotional experience for me and so very rewarding because I hadn't known these people before. The time we spent together taught me that I couldn't serve away all their problems, but I could serve in all the ways I knew how. I served to love that couple, and I loved to serve them.

As I ponder that experience, I'm worried it might sound

> AS WE LABOR
> SHOULDER TO
> SHOULDER, WE FEEL
> THE PRESENCE AND
> INFLUENCE OF THE
> HOLY GHOST, AND THAT
> HELPS US LEARN TO
> LOVE ONE ANOTHER.

like I'm boasting about good works. The truth is, many sisters helped, and every woman I know wants to serve in some way. Service is the one universal ingredient that brings people together. As we labor shoulder to shoulder, we feel the presence and influence of the Holy Ghost, and that helps us learn to love one another. Serving doesn't just help us see people we serve the way Christ does, it helps us see our service partners that way too. If a friend called me today and said she was struggling to get along with a woman in her neighborhood, or a relative, or a coworker, I'd counsel her to find an opportunity to serve that person. It works.

Sometimes our most significant service is the most unexpected and has nothing to do with a calling. It's simply a matter of having our eyes open. In the late 1990s I met a woman who'd survived a tough patch in her life. Before we met, she had suffered tragedy while on a family vacation. I can still hear her telling me the story for the first time.

They were driving the family station wagon, all the kids safely snuggled in the back. Suddenly she had an incredibly strong impression. She asked her husband to pull over, but he suggested they wait until the next exit. "No," she said. "Pull over now."

They did, and one of the children, a darling boy, was dead. He'd died of carbon monoxide poisoning. If they hadn't stopped, this precious family of five would have all perished.

We spoke at length about the tragedy and how sad she still felt. One afternoon, as we were looking at photos of her family, she said, "You know, Gail, I've never been able to do anything with all this. I would really love to put a scrapbook together about my boy's life."

I instinctively invited her over, and we spent months creating a large scrapbook about this little boy. He came alive on those pages right before our eyes. This small act closed a loop for her and gave her peace. Then she used the scrapbook to bring peace to her other kids, too. Even today the memory makes me cry. By donating a little bit of time, a scanner, and some supplies, I made a friend in that little boy. I look forward to meeting him in person on the other side.

———

That memory reminds me of another time in my life when I learned how to love by serving, and it all started with my favorite book: the Book of Mormon. Though there were not many nonmembers in our ward boundaries, there was one Catholic couple who lived across the street from a very good friend of mine. My friend was one of the happiest, most loving, most service-minded people I'd ever known. She understood perfectly this unbreakable bond between love and service.

One day she told me how sad she was to see that her neighbors, the kind Catholic couple, were moving. She said, "I've been meaning to give her a Book of Mormon for so long and now she's going to be gone. I can't let that happen. I can't let her leave without one."

My friend gave them the gift, and, I still don't know why, but for some reason, the family ended up staying put. Soon the wife started showing up at Relief Society. I was teaching then, and I could tell our new friend was soaking up the doctrines and principles of the gospel. One Sunday, she tearfully told me she wouldn't be able to attend for a while. Her husband wasn't well and she needed to be home with him on Sundays. She was genuinely devastated, and I grinned as I thought, "This might be the only time someone has shed a tear over missing a Gail Miller lesson."

I gave her a hug and told her I would love for her to come visit me during the week. "I'll teach you the lessons in my home. Would that work?"

She graciously accepted the offer, and once a week for about six months she came to my home. I retaught the previous Sunday's Relief Society lesson, whether I'd been the original teacher or not. We had some of the most spiritual experiences together on those special days. Eventually she was baptized, and a year later she went to the temple. I remember her saying that she didn't want to join the Church just for the women, she wanted to know the doctrine was true, and our one-on-one sessions had been helpful. I told her it wasn't me who had done that—I was simply the conduit of service.

A decade later her daughter committed suicide, and I was so grateful she had the gospel in her life to help her through that devastating time. I was thankful I had been placed in her life at the right time with the right spirit to serve her.

As of today, her husband is not a member, but he's a faithful man who is receptive to home teachers and attends church with her from time to time. What a tender mercy that all started with the gift of a Book of Mormon.

During this same time, Kim, who would later become my second husband, also lived in our ward boundaries. His home was on a quiet, dead-end street tucked into the mountainside. He also had a nonmember neighbor who'd been befriended by sisters in the ward. She had a tough life and did her best to hang on. She battled depression, a grueling work schedule, and the responsibility of raising two fine boys. Sadly, her life was also touched by suicide: Her husband had taken his life.

Unbelievably, after all this, one day her house caught fire. I'd developed a good rapport with her that had nothing to do with religion and everything to do with friendship. I was honored to mobilize a group of women to go down and tear out all the carpet, clean up the cabinets, and assist the men from the ward in doing their part. When we were done, Kim said to me, "Gail, when I saw you doing that for our nonmember friend, it made me wonder . . . what manner of woman is this?"

LOVE WITHOUT SERVICE ISN'T LOVE AT ALL. IT MIGHT BE ADMIRATION, BUT IT'S NOT LOVE.

What a humbling thing to hear, but I should have corrected him. "What manner of women are *these*?" Once again it was a team effort based on Christlike love. Because we'd learned to love her, we had no choice but to serve her. Love without service isn't love at all. It might be *admiration,* but it's not *love.*

If I'm being honest, I have to say it's impossible to imagine I would have served like this when I was wrapped up in my own life as a young mom or avoiding the Church altogether as a young adult. These experiences, which are not easy to share, helped me see that I've been surrounded my entire life by people who modeled the power of service. Perhaps to fully appreciate this principle, we all need to experience seasons of life when we're the recipients of service and other seasons when we're performing it as often as possible. At times we're the students, and at other times we're the teachers.

Surveying my own life, I see how the Lord put countless service mentors in my path for me to witness firsthand how to help when my time would come. I haven't done anything special, I've just been put in the right place at the right time to try my hand at what I've seen so many others do.

I loved serving as a Relief Society president for the lessons I learned and for the opportunities to serve. But we've all known many women who've performed these kinds of services, and many more, without ever serving in a leadership position. To me, they're the real heroes.

Years before his passing, Larry and I got to know a couple in our ward through his home-teaching assignment. The man wasn't particularly active, but that was fine with us. We really enjoyed being around them, and we all became great friends. Among our favorite things to do was unwind over dinner at a restaurant. Whenever we did, Larry always grabbed for the check. Picking up the tab was something small we could do because we knew the family didn't have means for many meals out. The tradition grew to whatever we might have been doing together; we always took care of the bill and didn't think twice.

One day when Larry wasn't around, the husband said to me, "Gail, we are thankful, but we can't keep taking from you. Please let us pay sometimes."

I told Larry the story, but the next time we were scheduled for dinner, he insisted once again that he would be paying. I pulled him aside and said, "Larry, you need to let him pay. He's got to serve too. He's got to feel that he's as valuable as you are." It presented a stark picture for us of exactly what it means to allow others to have the same opportunities that we have. It's important to know both sides of the love and service coin and to be both a gracious giver *and* a gracious receiver.

It's tempting to think that accepting service makes us look weak and incapable. But when I've felt or witnessed this, I've been reminded of the Savior allowing His feet to be washed by the penitent woman. He didn't need it, *she did,* and He loved her so much that He allowed it.

When we close our eyes in a private moment, we might imagine someone in our lives who's living in the shadows, a shy soul who needs an opportunity to step into the light.

When that happens, let's give them a call, ask for a favor, give them a chance to serve us or to work alongside us. We'll be amazed at the love we feel by witnessing someone other than ourselves receiving the unique blessings that come from service.

Though I've learned much from the moments I have served others, I've learned even more when others have served me. When my son Roger died, friends perceived my grief and sent simple notes of encouragement. When Larry died, an entire community mourned with me.

> THOUGH I'VE LEARNED MUCH FROM THE MOMENTS I HAVE SERVED OTHERS, I'VE LEARNED EVEN MORE WHEN OTHERS HAVE SERVED ME.

My needs were simple. I didn't require help with cleaning or cooking or rides here and there. Instead, when I needed it most, someone served me with a hug, a treat, or a prayer on my behalf. You might even be one of those people who saw the value of simple service by paying condolences at a funeral, or when you saw me at a Jazz game, or standing in line at the store. Believe me—those moments mattered. They lifted me.

One of my favorite memories of being served started as just a thank you but has become so much more. After the second of my husband Kim's two house fires, his family hand tied a quilt for me. Both of our first spouses were still living, and I didn't think much of it then, but over time I see that Kim's family wasn't just thanking me for my service to them as a Relief Society president, they were serving me right back with a special remembrance that has stayed with me ever since. The blanket remains a link to Kim's dear wife and that cherished time of my life. Who could have possibly known that one day both our spouses would pass and Kim and I would marry? Only the Lord.

It's possible that one of the greatest obstacles to love and service is our predisposition to judge. I wonder how many moments of service we miss because we've judged the person, family, or cause to be unworthy.

"She's not active, I'm not sure I can serve her with a glad heart."

"She could clean her house herself, why would I join the service project?"

"He smokes and smells like alcohol, let someone else help him."

Even when I was young, this attitude troubled me. I was taught to believe the Lord is the judge, yet we're quick sometimes to assume that role from the Savior as if we think we're more qualified. But the real lesson is that while He *is* the judge, He serves us anyway. So, then, how much more need have *we* to serve?

We might be quick to react negatively to things we disagree with or would do differently. We're quick to compare and judge others against ourselves. We're so willing to compare one imperfect person—*them*—to another imperfect person—*us*. That's like picking up two equally dirty dishes out of the sink and choosing which you'd rather use. Dirty is dirty. We all need service of one kind or another at various times in our lives.

Consider also that serving others at any age doesn't mean we're obligated to take them home and develop a lifelong friendship. Maybe we will, but we must not assign ourselves more than is needed. You might meet a new woman on your street who's very different from you. You could have diverse interests, schedules, and backgrounds. But you might have something that could enrich her life, or vice versa. By serving her, even in small and simple ways, you will see walls come down. Even if you never share a book, a ball game, or a barbecue together, that neighbor will still always know where your heart is.

Throughout my life I've mulled over how hard it is to

serve and love others when you can't serve and love yourself. When I feel that way, I like to remind myself of a few simple truths. We are children of God, created in His image and always on His mind. Our Savior's love for us is linked to His greatest act of service, the Atonement. How much does Jesus Christ love us? He bled for us. How much does He want us home again? He died and was resurrected for you and me.

Because of His example and the examples of so many who live as His disciples, I've learned to love to serve and I serve to love. I know these inseparable principles will draw all of us closer to the Savior.

Friendship Is a Choice

Yes, You Can (and Should)
Pick Your Friends

I received my patriarchal blessing along with my Primary classmates when I was nine years old. My teacher felt it was important for us to receive the blessings that were prepared for each of us by a loving Heavenly Father as early as possible. She explained that a patriarchal blessing could serve as a road map for life so we could prepare ourselves for the unique blessings our Father in Heaven had in store for us.

I knew this was an important step, but I didn't comprehend it very well. I'm not sure anyone does when they are nine years old. After a decade or two and hundreds of times reading and pondering my blessing, I can now see how it did provide a road map to having more courage when I needed it the most.

One paragraph of my blessing has always stood out. I was counseled to seek for the companionship of those who would be uplifting to me and to set a proper example for others. I've considered that often throughout my life. I've discovered through my experiences that the Lord is the ultimate source of all things uplifting. Those words resonated with me. Of all the things available to me in that blessing, the one about good companions seemed within my reach even as a child. I committed to myself that no matter what, I would hang on to that piece of heavenly advice to choose good friends and be a good friend.

THE COST TO ASSOCIATE WITH PEOPLE WHO CAN BRING SOMETHING GOOD TO OUR LIVES IS WORTH THE EFFORT.

I've observed time and time again that the cost to associate with people who can bring something good to our lives is worth the effort, while the cost to associate with those who tear us down is definitely *not* worth the price. Good begets good, and as we look for those people, we spiritually gravitate towards them. In no time, we'll see others gravitating towards us for the same reason.

During the summer between grade school and junior high, a new girl named Grethe—pronounced "Greta"— moved into my close-knit neighborhood. She was from what seemed to me like the farthest corner of the earth. Denmark! I'd never actually had a friend who spoke a different language, but I felt an instant connection to her because my grandparents were from Denmark and my mother sometimes spoke Danish with my aunts and uncles. Grethe was the only member of her family who spoke English.

I wanted to help this new girl adjust as she was trying to make a home in what was to her a foreign land. Despite our vastly different backgrounds, we shared the same deep desire for a friendship.

Our friendship grew quickly, and she fit right in with our little group. Our entire universe covered six square blocks. Oh, how I loved those years. We shared all our secret hopes and dreams. We were content to play hopscotch or jacks on the sidewalk, or to play ball with any kind of ball we could find. In the evenings all the neighbor kids would gather to play games like kick the can, Red Rover, and hide-and-seek until the sun set and it was too dark to see. It's hard to remember in today's digital society how an after-school game of Red Rover with all your friends can make more connections and memories than Facebook ever could.

When we moved from sixth grade into seventh, Grethe and I were talking with another friend who expressed how excited she was for the opportunity to hang out and befriend the popular girls as she moved to junior high. She wanted to be popular and had determined that was the way to do it. I was stunned. "Why would you care about that?" I asked.

Honestly, I wasn't being a smart aleck. I couldn't understand why being popular was so important to her. I didn't know or even care what being popular was *supposed* to look like. I just knew how I felt when I was around a good friend. That was what was important to me.

In fact, I was shocked the first time it was pointed out to me that someone didn't like me. Up to that point it had never occurred to me that someone might not like another person. One of my friends revealed that another classmate didn't like me and didn't want to be my friend. "What?" I thought. "How can they not like me? What's not to like about me?" It was shocking, not because I was so special the world was obligated to adore me, but because I couldn't think of any reasons why a person wouldn't like someone. I was too young to really understand that people could even generate those feelings. I enjoyed everyone and assumed that was how the world worked.

I was hurt, but rather than shying away, I decided right then that I would work harder to be a good friend. Since then I've been determined to love people for who they are and accept that it's perfectly fine if not everyone appreciates me.

When the new person in the neighborhood or the newly elected chair of the homeowners' association doesn't seem to care for us, we can wilt and pull our petals up over our faces and say, "I'm not going to go out in the world anymore." Or, we can respond with resolve to be better. "Okay. Maybe I can try harder on my end, or maybe I can move toward other people I have more in common with."

What we can't do is judge those who keep us at arm's length. And we absolutely must not quit being true to ourselves. I've always loved the opening lines of the poem "Myself" by Edgar Guest.

> *I have to live with myself and so*
> *I want to be fit for myself to know.*
> *I want to be able as days go by,*
> *Always to look myself straight in the eye;*
> *I don't want to stand with the setting sun*
> *And hate myself for the things I have done.*

Think about it. A friend who requires you to be someone other than who you are isn't interested in a friendship at all. What that person wants is a performance.

Decades later, Grethe and I remain close. We don't see each other as often as we used to, but when we do, it's like we're still walking back and forth on our quiet street swapping stories and divulging dreams. I love Grethe just as much as I did in 1955, and we both believe that our friendship has

A FRIEND WHO REQUIRES YOU TO BE SOMEONE OTHER THAN WHO YOU ARE ISN'T INTERESTED IN A FRIENDSHIP AT ALL. WHAT THAT PERSON WANTS IS A PERFORMANCE.

endured because it's based on principles of trust and truth. Friendships might be sparked by geography, but they last by loyalty.

As I grew and moved from place to place, I recognized that if I kept my promise of choosing to surround myself with people who inspired me, the Lord would reward me with a friend or two placed in my path for a very specific reason. Such friends have taught me, loved me, served me, and allowed *me* to serve *them*. When it's been time to move on, for whatever reason, I've never gotten so far away that I cannot see them in the rearview mirror.

My mother used to repeat these lines from the well-known Joseph Parry poem: "Make new friends, but keep the old. The new are silver, the old are gold." She was right. Everyone in your life is of worth, whether your connection is daily, weekly, or via an annual glossy Christmas card.

Sometimes when I see from a distance a young mother struggling, I find myself praying she has a good friend like Grethe waiting on the other side of a call or a text or across the street in her neighborhood. Everyone needs friends during each season of life to relate to and to help them tackle the daily struggles they each identify with. When we were kids, our friends were kids. As young adults, most of our friends were probably young adults too. There's no better resource for a first-time mom to lean on than someone living the same challenges.

I think one of the reasons women need close friendships more than men seem to is because they do so many things that don't come with manuals. No matter how well you prepare, there is no one who can really teach you how to be a mother. Nobody gives you a step-by-step checklist for most of the circumstances you're going to be confronted with. We all need someone to confide in, to bounce ideas off of, and to help us understand that together, we're going to make it. Who hasn't ever observed someone else and thought, "Oh, that's how they did it. Maybe that will work for me"? It just might. My mother told me more than once that parenthood

I THINK ONE OF THE REASONS WOMEN NEED CLOSE FRIENDSHIPS MORE THAN MEN SEEM TO IS BECAUSE THEY DO SO MANY THINGS THAT DON'T COME WITH MANUALS.

is the one job that by the time you are experienced, you are unemployed—and she had nine children.

———

Not long ago on a Sunday morning I was sitting in the cultural hall in a new ward for a combined priesthood and Relief Society meeting. We'd been discussing friendship and fellowship in the ward and how easy it is to feel disconnected. We had been in the ward for only a few months, and I was still feeling somewhat alone and missing the good friends I had left in my previous ward. I privately wondered, "Why am I not feeling happy here? Why am I not feeling comfortable in this new place?"

In that moment, I knew what was missing. I needed to find somebody I could connect to. I couldn't sit around and wait. As I listened to the discussion, my mind wandered to what it was about my last ward that had made me feel comfortable. I realized that to have a friend, I needed to be a friend. I needed to make it known that I was eager to be a part of this new ward. Without much thought—which was a good thing or I might have talked myself out of it—I raised my hand and said, "I'm new in this ward, and I need a friend."

I think I got a dozen calls that afternoon.

I'm no friendship expert, but I think admitting I felt alone and needed a friend might have resonated with others in the congregation that day. Those calls reminded me that I needed to *be* that friend too. I want to be the friend others need, and I sense that as I live that way, I'll attract the kind of people I want to associate with. I promise the same is true for you too.

When my family moved from Colorado back to Utah, and Larry and I bought our first dealership, I met a woman in our new neighborhood who had an instant impact on me. We connected with our first conversation. Over the years we worked together in several Church assignments. We had a lot in common. We were about the same age, and our children were in the same grades in school. I intently observed how she lived her life and appreciated what I saw. She was always dedicated to doing the right thing. I wanted to be as committed as she was, but I thought that was out of reach for me at the time.

One day, as she shared a spiritual experience and some guidance she'd received, I looked her in the eyes and said, "I would really like to have that kind of spiritual guidance in my life, but I never do."

She smiled. "Gail, I'm sure you *do* have that in your life. You just don't recognize it yet."

I thought about that bold statement and decided that if such guidance were really available to me, then it was up to me to grab it and make it visible and bring it into my life.

I still have work to do in that regard, but my ability to feel and recognize the Spirit and discern the influence of the Holy Ghost is better because of that friend. She made me better without even trying.

During another season of my life, when I wondered aloud to Larry why no one ever called me, he smiled and gave me this blunt advice: "Sweetheart, why don't you call them?"

It wasn't just advice, it was Larry's way of life. To this day, I have no idea how he accomplished so much every day, and not exclusively in business. He wrote personal notes, made phone calls, stopped on his way from one important commitment to another to listen to someone's problems. When he would download his day, I'd ask, "How do you have time for that? Where do you get that many hours in a day?"

Even beyond that, I asked how he could even think of these acts of kindness in the first place. What was it that jogged his mind to think, 'I should call this person. I should send flowers. I should jot down a quick card'?

I used to think it was wired in his DNA, but over time and a life of teaching by example, I learned it wasn't second nature. He had trained himself to do those things. Caring was a purposeful skill, and it endeared him to people and nourished friendships. It's just another one of those instances when the more you serve, the more you love, and the more you love, the more connected you are. The more connected you are, the greater the opportunity to make a difference in someone's life.

I learned from Larry, an exceptionally gifted mentor, but I also learned from many friends who became my teachers. I admire how deftly someone has shown me how to do certain things and what's worked for them. We have to be careful, of course, in this approach. We can't boast about having all the answers, but what a blessing for a friend to say in a delicate, loving way, "May I share my own experience?"

Or, "This is how I handled that."

Or, even more simply, "Have you thought about this?"

Instead of overpowering with our self-described more experienced opinions, we can take the initiative and look for ways to be helpful. It's all about the connections. We can do so much with our friendships; our influence can be like those ripples on the water that roll farther than our eyes could ever see.

No honest discussion of friendship is complete without a word or two on what might be called "relationship guilt." Is there anyone who hasn't felt overwhelmed at feeling the need to be a friend to every living creature? I've sure felt that way.

There is a distinction between being friendly and opening up your heart in a vulnerable way to someone you've learned to love. We must remember that everyone has eternal value and a divine nature, even those who are completely different from us. But the commandment is to love one another, not to have lunch with one another every Tuesday at noon.

> THE COMMANDMENT IS TO LOVE ONE ANOTHER, NOT TO HAVE LUNCH WITH ONE ANOTHER EVERY TUESDAY AT NOON.

Recently I've been working on a commission to address the homelessness crisis in Salt Lake City and surrounding communities. One of the messages that gets lost in the conversation is that these are real people with real thoughts and feelings and emotions and needs and desires, just like you and me. They've just been treated differently, or had unique trials, or made poor choices. That doesn't mean we should shun them. Nor does it mean we can pull every single one into our lives and pledge, "I will be your friend." It's not possible.

Instead, we can serve them with all our hearts. We can volunteer time, donate to worthy causes, say "hello" on the street, and smile back with the light of Christ. And if we can't give anything but a smile and a prayer on their behalf, we shouldn't feel guilty for our efforts. The Lord always accepts our sincere offering.

Other experiences in business and volunteerism have

taught me to acknowledge the nearly endless kinds of love. I've been privileged to work alongside men and women of different faiths, political stripes, sexual preferences, education levels, and residences from nearly every zip code in the West. I've learned countless lessons from them and I'm honored to share time and find common ground. But I feel completely at peace about my inability to share my entire life with every single one of them. Sharing goodness, as we're counseled, is not the same thing as sharing a deep, personal friendship.

So what about the deepest, most personal friendships? Whenever I have the opportunity to speak or give advice on business, I invite the audience members to make their spouses their very best friends and most important partners—no exceptions. Marriage is our most complex, important relationship and it cannot be replaced.

I've shared that Larry and I did not have a perfect marriage, and during our rocky times we wondered if our partnership would survive. Looking back, I credit our friendship and desire to communicate as the key to our ultimately successful relationship. As best friends, we talked about everything: the house, our faith, our family, and the business. Though I wasn't in the office, Larry never made a significant business decision without me. He constantly walked me through his decision-making process and sought my opinion.

Now, that's not to say our communications were always on the same frequency. Larry and I cherished honesty, and it was a foundation of our relationship, but sometimes I was reminded that, as the popular book says, women might be from Venus, but sometimes it feels like men are from an unknown galaxy beyond any telescope.

I wasn't laughing then, but one memory makes me smile today. Perhaps like some of you, I gained baby weight that I never lost. In fact, I probably gained ten pounds with each of my five pregnancies. Let's be honest: Forty years after having my last child, I don't think I'm even allowed to call it baby weight anymore.

But one evening I was complaining—or communicating—about how heavy I was. "Larry, I've never weighed this much in my life."

Without so much as a breath, Larry responded, "Well, maybe your hormones are out of whack."

Ouch. I said I appreciated honesty, but not *that much* honesty. It wasn't exactly what a woman wants to hear, was it? What I longed for was for him to put his arms around me and say, "You're beautiful and I love you just the way you are."

I didn't love him any less, but I did find myself imagining how that moment might have played out with one of my dear female friends. She would have hugged me tight and said, "Oh, but you're fine! You're beautiful to me and I love you!"

Women just have a different approach to friendship—and a few other things. But when your best friend is your spouse, you breathe deep, forgive, and count your blessings.

As much as I believe in sincere communication, I also maintain that loyalty in friendships means never speaking ill when you're apart. It's a trap that's easy to fall into, but your secrets with your spouse belong there. Your concerns about friends, no matter how well founded, belong within your friendship. I cringe when I hear husbands or wives taking shots at their spouses or when friends smile when facing one another but become judge and jury when apart. I have learned that the best way to nourish any friendship, especially during a tough patch, is to never have a conversation *about* a friend that you wouldn't have *with* that friend. I suspect you've seen that kind of loyalty rewarded more than once.

Though I haven't always been the best about maintaining friendships with

> THE BEST WAY TO NOURISH ANY FRIENDSHIP, ESPECIALLY DURING A TOUGH PATCH, IS TO NEVER HAVE A CONVERSATION ABOUT A FRIEND THAT YOU WOULDN'T HAVE WITH THAT FRIEND.

people who've moved away, I hold onto a desire to see them and to reconnect. Wouldn't it be wonderful to live your life in such a way that you had no regrets? Just think about having someone from any era of your life pass you on the street or join the same line in the grocery store and be able to feel completely at peace. I'm grateful to have learned that lesson on the sleepy streets of my childhood. I'm not an example of perfection on this topic or any other, but I feel confident that I've never done anything or said anything that would inhibit the Spirit should I cross paths again with any of my old friends.

Not long ago my husband Kim and I were at dinner in a local restaurant when a man came walking around a corner and approached our table. "You look familiar," he said.

I looked back at him and said, "You look familiar too." He reminded me who he was and we reconnected the dots: We had attended high school together. Soon his wife joined us, then another couple they were eating with, and we made connections everywhere. In just a few minutes we had retraced our steps to a sweet man who'd given Kim's late wife a blessing near the end of her life.

What a joy, I thought, that we'd all been good to one another all those years ago. We hadn't been best friends, but we'd been kind to one another.

For the last decade or so I've belonged to a very special group of twelve women. We call ourselves The Bucket Club, and our mission is to gather once a month and fill each other's buckets. We rotate from one home to another and spend our time together focusing on becoming a little bit better than we were the month before by sharing enriching experiences.

When Larry died, I was the first of the group to lose a spouse. Their friendship was priceless. They were so kind with their questions, and because we'd built a foundation of truth and trust, and because we'd chosen one another as friends, and because we shared values, the dialogue was always supportive and uplifting.

"What's it like to lose your husband? How do you feel? What are you going through? What's life like now? How can I help?"

We talk about our children, but only to lift them. We talk about our husbands, but only to praise them. We talk about our faith, but only to grow it. What we've never done in over ten years of meetings is violate the rules of friendship. Every month we count our blessings and remind one another that we'll never make it through this life alone. We always have to have someone to go to or lean on, or who wants to lean on us. I might lean today, maybe even tomorrow, and their turn to lean on me will surely come. I hope these friends have learned a little from me, and I know I've learned a lot from them through the enriching experiences we have shared.

Sometimes when I drive away from a gathering of the Bucket Club, I remember the old adage that we are the average of the five people we associate with the most. I hope that's not quite right. I will be a happy daughter of God if at the judgment bar I have become the average of those twelve divine friends.

Although I can't guarantee this concept will work for everyone, I do recommend gathering as often as reasonable and practical with friends who remind you of the Savior. Maybe your group is less formal, maybe it's more organized than ours, but I promise that regularly filling your bucket to the brim with goodness makes your journey much lighter.

I don't know, maybe friendship is even more simple than I've described. It's about kindness. Listening to the Holy Ghost. Being ourselves and becoming the best version of ourselves. Forgiving easily. Playing hopscotch. Sharing our hopes and dreams. And, naturally, it's about following Christ, the most perfect Friend we'll ever know in this life or the next.

Lost and Found

How Death Helps Us Find Ourselves

My parents were preparing for the birth of their eighth child, and I couldn't have been more excited. Because I had been so interested in where babies come from and in the mysteries of life that a new baby brings with it, my mother had tenderly prepared me for the arrival of this new little person. She carefully taught me with lessons of the gospel about where we come from, why we're here, and where we are going. She explained that this baby was living with our Heavenly Parents while she was waiting to come to earth to live with our family. I envied her life in such a beautiful place and marveled that she was in the presence of relatives whom I had seen only in pictures. I was looking forward to being her big sister and sharing my world with her.

However, during her birth something went terribly wrong, and my new baby sister, Kathleen Marie, was not allowed to stay with our family. Because of a complication during the birth, she had a lack of oxygen and lived only eleven hours.

Kathleen Marie was a beautiful baby. I remember standing on my tiptoes at her funeral, staring into her miniature casket, admiring her dark hair, and hearing my mother whisper in my ear, "She looks just like you did."

It was a sad time, of course, but my parents consoled and comforted me so well that I didn't feel disconnected from this sister I never got to hold or play with. They taught me and my siblings that dying is a sad but natural part of life, and explained that Kathleen was in a better place with our Heavenly Father.

In the years since saying good-bye to my tiny sister, I've had many experiences with death, and I've learned that it can be a lovely thing. No, not easy, but somehow still beautiful.

A year after Kathleen's death, my mother had another baby. By then I understood that my parents weren't replacing Kathleen; she was back where she'd come from. She was with

> I'VE HAD MANY EXPERIENCES WITH DEATH, AND I'VE LEARNED THAT IT CAN BE A LOVELY THING. NO, NOT EASY, BUT SOMEHOW STILL BEAUTIFUL.

God, and we would now welcome a new baby to our family—this time a brother.

Looking in the rearview mirror, I recognize it's my religious beliefs of life before life and life after life that soothe the sting of loss. We don't just live *after* death, we live *before* we come to earth, and once we get here we should live every single day to its fullest.

I didn't have to stand on my tiptoes at my next funeral. My parents were needed in California to counsel with my older brother, who was going through a divorce, but they didn't have enough money to make the trip. Since I had a job, I offered to pay for it if we could make it a family vacation, too.

My mom, my dad, my younger sister and brother, and I piled into our old 1953 Ford that emitted heavy smoke and required us to pull over and refill it with oil along the way. But we had a prayer in our hearts that we would get there safely—and we did. It was our first vacation in nine years and it was quite an adventure.

We arrived in Sacramento, California, safely but while there, my dad suffered a serious stroke. It was a challenging time, especially being so far from home, but we relied on the

Lord for strength and felt His blessings. After Dad had spent a few months in the hospital in San Francisco, Mom was allowed to bring him home to Salt Lake, but he was still very ill. For the next two years she lovingly cared for him in our home. One Sunday morning he had a relapse and had to be readmitted to the hospital.

That evening, with my wedding two weeks away, I sat at the kitchen table addressing wedding invitations. My mother called from the hospital and asked me to come up for a visit. "He's not doing so well," she said.

I couldn't spare the time, I told her. I needed to finish addressing my invitations before my evening shift at the telephone company. As soon as I said the words, I knew I had made the wrong decision, but I didn't change my plans. I reported for work at 5:00 p.m., and at 6:05 p.m. my supervisor told me the bad news—my father had passed away. I left immediately and went to the hospital to be with my mother.

My mother said that in Dad's final seconds, he looked up toward the ceiling, his eyes opened wide as if he were seeing a loved one from a time long ago, and he smiled with a look of peace on his face. She was sure it was his dear mother, who had died when he was just twelve years old. I tried to console myself with the lessons I had learned when my sister died. He wasn't dead; he was in heaven with loved ones.

My father was gone. I wish I could say my regrets were gone too. Like anyone would, I've always wished I had put down that silly pen, perhaps called in sick, and made a final trip to his bedside. But I truly had no idea he would die that night.

When I'm tempted to feel guilty for not being at his bedside, I remember how hard I worked to honor him while he was alive. I couldn't let a single regret overshadow a lifetime of loving, respecting, and serving my dear father.

I missed him, naturally, and I wish we'd had more time together, but my dad didn't belong to me any more than any of my other loved ones who've passed away did. They have gone home to something more glorious than our imperfect world can offer. It's hard for me to feel the sadness in that.

With my wedding to Larry less than two weeks away, there were some relatives who thought I should postpone it. I respected their opinions—I still do—but in counseling with my mother I was convinced I should press forward. I realized the only way my father could have attended my wedding was from the other side of the veil. I know he was there and rejoicing with us.

It was a bittersweet day. Almost everyone who was invited came to console my mother, then to celebrate with me and Larry. There were plenty of tears of all kinds, and if I had to,

I'd do it the same way all over again. Daddy's little girl was getting married! What a perfect way to honor my father and to lift up my mother. It was an important mile marker in my own journey home.

Years later I drew on these experiences as Relief Society president when I helped with many funerals of dear sisters and even spoke at a few. The truth is that I have come to enjoy funerals. I appreciate the unique spirit that accompanies the music, the prayers, and the talks. I love hearing the wonderful things said about the departed ones we mourn. Sometimes my mind wanders and I wonder, "What will my family and friends say about me?"

Each funeral I've attended has taught me even more about how important it is to grieve in our own way, and not like someone else. Even as a child, I felt the need to say the right thing to someone who'd lost a loved one, even if it felt awkward. I discovered that as uncomfortable as it might be, people who are suffering appreciate the opportunity to talk about their loss, and it isn't helpful for me to share my experiences when they're the ones in need of comfort. When someone is caught in the fog of grief, the last thing that person wants to hear is, "Oh, I know exactly how you're feeling. I've been through that."

All of us have probably said something like that, and even

followed up by telling our own painful stories. But people want to know that we're in the moment with them, that we feel their sorrow, that we're suffering with them or at least acknowledging what they're going through without comparing our pain with theirs. Letting those who are grieving have time, space, and opportunity to share their feelings and sorrows is helpful to them. If they don't want to talk, that's fine too. At least you've let them know that you're there for them. What they appreciate most is a pure, two-word message: "I care."

Leading the Relief Society, I had several opportunities to serve during times of grief. One sister in my ward who was from the Philippines developed a serious heart problem. After her doctors inserted a stent, it became infected, and her health continued to worsen. I stayed in close contact with her husband, reported back to the ward, and counseled with the bishop about how we could help this couple. One Sunday I took a variety of cards to church, gave them to the sisters, and invited them to share their thoughts with the woman and her family. She was too ill for visitors, so I gathered up the

> PEOPLE WANT TO KNOW THAT WE'RE IN THE MOMENT WITH THEM, THAT WE FEEL THEIR SORROW, THAT WE'RE SUFFERING WITH THEM.

personalized notes and delivered them to her. She wasn't able to recover from the infection but was touched by the knowledge that her Relief Society sisters were praying for her. She passed away the following week. I believe those messages helped comfort her husband and helped him with his grieving, too.

Sometimes our experiences with death are a little more public—like when my husband passed away. Larry H. Miller was a man with a big name and an even bigger heart. Some might think that he worked himself to death building a billion-dollar company with thousands of employees. Not me. I think he lived himself to death. Yes, he worked hard, perhaps harder than any entrepreneur ever. But he also loved, served, taught, and led others with everything he had during his journey on earth.

Larry did not die suddenly. When he was first diagnosed with diabetes, he refused to believe it. It took him several years to accept the fact that he had a serious disease. His personality allowed him to believe he could overcome anything and everything—that he could heal himself through sheer willpower. Unfortunately, diabetes doesn't respond that way.

Diabetes is a silent illness that causes damage before you're even aware. By the time you recognize or accept it, you could be well down the road to irreversible damage. That was precisely what happened to my late husband. When the doctor explained how the disease could progress and prescribed medication, my soft-hearted but hard-headed husband said to him, "I don't like how I feel when I take that pill. I'm going to quit taking it." He honestly thought he would overcome deadly sickness by mental toughness. But you can't imagine an injection; you need to actually take it. Believe it or not, by the time Larry needed insulin, his doctor had to give himself a shot just to prove to Larry it wouldn't hurt!

As for me, I didn't want to nag or pester. I once said to a nurse friend of mine, "Larry is a big boy, and if he wants to take care of himself, he will. He's got to have the courage to do this."

The friend looked in my eyes and said, "Oh, no, no, no, Gail. You have to do everything you can to help him. Diabetes is the worst way to die." And she was right! Thankfully, one day Larry finally realized the doctor was right and began taking insulin.

The next phase of our lives was like a roller-coaster ride I would not wish on anyone. The last year of Larry's life could be a medical documentary on the effects of diabetes. He was in the hospital, then out, suffered a heart attack, had his legs amputated, and developed sepsis. Doctors said he died five times during those final months, but no one was surprised that Larry wanted to negotiate the terms of his good-bye.

He was afflicted with an incurable disease called calciphylaxis. When he knew he would not get better, he made the decision to discontinue dialysis. He said, "I want to go home." Our dear friend Elder M. Russell Ballard of the Quorum of the Twelve Apostles gave him a powerful blessing. With the Lord's authority threading the words together, he said, "Larry, you need to think about leaving this world and start preparing to go to the other side." Immediately, a calmness settled in the room and upon Larry. His anxiety was gone.

We knew he would live only a few more days without dialysis. I immediately gathered our family together. Our daughter, Karen, suggested we do something we hadn't done in decades: have a sleepover. The kids and grandkids gathered around our bed with sleeping bags, and we set up a television and an old VCR so we could watch home videos. Some of the footage was brand-new to the grandchildren, and the evening presented an interesting scene. They had the opportunity to learn things about their grandfather they'd never known, and Larry was living some family memories he hadn't always been there to experience in person. It was a sweet time.

In his final days and hours, Larry had private

conversations with every family member, the contents of which are too special and sacred to share. I'll just say that, like any self-proclaimed workaholic, he had a few regrets about opportunities missed. But he was also filled with love and awe at who his children and grandchildren had become and the wonderful friendships he had made.

The funeral was surreal and comforting. The outpouring of love from our Church, friends, and business associates was something I will never forget. Thomas S. Monson, President of The Church of Jesus Christ of Latter-day Saints and Larry's good friend, attended the service and shared kind memories of their friendship.

When the buzz died down and I settled into my new normal without Larry, I found myself thankful for our preparations. We had been able to discuss anything and everything, and I cannot recommend that strongly enough. You can't think of everything you need to know before a spouse dies, but we had prepared as well as we could and had been doing so for years. We had discussed money, the children, my life

> YOU CAN'T THINK OF EVERYTHING YOU NEED TO KNOW BEFORE A SPOUSE DIES, BUT WE HAD PREPARED AS WELL AS WE COULD AND HAD BEEN DOING SO FOR YEARS.

without him, property, the business, and his funeral. I knew where most of the important things were and what my first steps would be when he wasn't there to walk with me.

I did much of my mourning during his illness before he died. Because we knew it was coming, I lived at his side, asking questions and sharing memories. When your loved one is gone, you can't just go into the next room and ask a question or spend time together. Those are the things that you really have to do while the person is alive.

Going on without Larry was an interesting change because I had spent most of my life with him, all the way back to our teens. Our lives were interconnected in every way. After his death I tried to be realistic. I said to myself, "I need to find more courage than ever. I must learn how to live my life on my own without Larry to lean on." I thought it would take me about a year to figure out how to do that. But here I am, still interconnected. You never just cut ties. You still have all of what you had before, yet you also have the life you're currently trying to plan for. Death is not an end.

Even though I knew what I would see, the first time I walked into his office and stared at the papers and notes, I marveled at how it looked like he'd be back any second. That was when it really hit me, when the finality struck that we were separated for a time and I could not ask that last, lingering question. But seeing that preparation, that attention to detail, was comforting. Everyone knew how dedicated Larry was to work, and how he lived his whole life to create, help, grow, and serve. When it came time for him to prepare to go to the other side, he'd been just as dedicated to the exit.

When the calls and visits stopped, I turned to his writings. I went to his desk and looked at all the papers. I especially studied the yellow legal pads because I knew they held personal notes. I devoured it all. Then I went to his journals and letters. They helped heal me because it was a close connection, even though he wasn't there. It allowed me to say good-bye in my own time and in my own way.

I confess that I was grateful for some private time. That might sound strange because we've always heard, "They're going to need somebody after the funeral, when everybody's gone." But my life was so busy and so intense with him that in the peacefulness of the home we'd built together, I was grateful to have some quiet time for things I had never had time for before.

Make no mistake, I cried plenty, and I make no apologies for that. Crying is a healthy expression. I've always recognized that it's normal to have intense feelings and it's good to share them openly and honestly with God, family, and trusted friends. I took the time to write each of my children a letter.

I wanted to comfort them. I wanted them to know that I was there for them and I was still going to be their parent. It's important to be there for your children, even adult children, because loss is so personal. You don't have to solve all their problems, and they have to experience their own grieving, but I think it's crucial for them to know that you have common feelings. Share memories, especially happy ones. Remind one another you won't get over this in a minute or two. Take time to sort out your feelings, figure out where you're going, and plan how you're going to get there.

Some people talk of feeling waves of grief after losing a loved one. For me, it was waves of reality. This was real. It was so final. It was very stark. Today I look at that same desk and it's sterile and clean. His body takes up no space; it's nothing. But his spirit, my spirit, and your spirits, they take up a lot of space.

WE CAN FEEL BOTH SADNESS AND PEACE AT THE SAME TIME. THEY'RE NOT MUTUALLY EXCLUSIVE.

Maybe one of the most important things I learned from Larry's passing was that we can feel both sadness and peace at the same time. They're not mutually exclusive. We can grieve while we appreciate the joy these dear souls brought into our lives. Sure, we're here, they're there, and we can't do anything about that. But grief is the price we pay for the loss of someone we love.

———

Until recently, I'm not sure I'd ever stopped to think how unusual it is to have experienced so many kinds of grief and so many kinds of passing. I lost my sister less than a full day after her arrival. My father died at fifty-six. Larry passed far too young, at sixty-four, after many health challenges.

My mother? She died at the age of ninety-five after living a quiet, anonymous life. She was a righteous woman from her first day to her last. She had a tremendous impact on everyone who knew her, but her world was small. She wasn't appearing on the news or ESPN, or speaking at fund-raisers. All she did was live and exert nearly a hundred years' worth of positive influence. Everyone she encountered learned something good. She had an almost insatiable desire to teach and help those around her. Weighing less than seventy pounds and hobbled by Parkinson's disease, she was ready to go when it was her time. No regrets. Nothing left undone. My time caring for her in those final years was spiritual and sacred.

The one kind of death we all pray to never navigate is the passing of a child. Unfortunately, my turn came when I lost my son Roger in an accident while he was traveling in the

Midwest. I was devastated when I got the news, and I feel the pain of losing my child every day, but I'm grateful that he is with his father in a better place.

Though obviously not a public a figure the way Larry was, Roger was like him in many ways. They had a close relationship. He also worked hard and lived a life of service. Roger was just forty-four when he passed. He left behind a wonderful wife and nine children who love him dearly. He wasn't perfect, of course, but he was good. He lived well and was loved by those who knew him.

It's tempting to compare these experiences, and maybe you've done the same in your own life. With both of my parents, there was time to prepare for their deaths. The same was true with Larry. But with Roger, he was there one day and gone the next. I recall how hard it was waiting for his body to arrive in Utah. It wasn't until I stood there and saw him that reality sank in.

There is danger in comparisons, though. It really makes no difference: loss of siblings, parents, spouses, or children. A loss is a loss. Is it harder to lose a spouse than a child? Is it harder to lose a leg than an arm? I've learned that it's meaningless to make comparisons when the plan isn't ours, it's God's.

I think when you get to that point of loss in your life, if you have a belief system, you realize death is really only the next step in a glorious progression. I believe with all my heart in the Resurrection. My faith assures me that all the impurities we experience here will one day be gone and we'll be made whole.

My journey, every unexpected step, has taught me to believe that Christ lives and that death is just a blink. With each loss, no matter how painful, I see more clearly that death demonstrates how much our Father in Heaven loves each and every one of us. Without it, there is no return to Him.

I've spent many hours considering loss and sorrow and finding myself through the grieving process. Sometimes friends or family ask if I have regrets. Would I do things differently? Would I pray away my grief? The answer often surprises people: no. It's not that I want to endure any of it again—I doubt any of us would—but I cannot deny that experiencing loss can enable us to find ourselves and our place in God's patient plan for us.

> WITH EACH LOSS, NO MATTER HOW PAINFUL, I SEE MORE CLEARLY THAT DEATH DEMONSTRATES HOW MUCH OUR FATHER IN HEAVEN LOVES EACH AND EVERY ONE OF US. WITHOUT IT, THERE IS NO RETURN TO HIM.

Don't Wait on Patience

Patience Is a Verb

I often reminisce about my childhood in the Marmalade District of Salt Lake. I was the sixth of nine children, and we were taught inside the walls of our humble home to be honest, truthful, chaste, virtuous, and good to everyone. We learned these principles and many more by trial and error, but maybe none more than patience. Our meager circumstances were the perfect laboratory for learning to be patient.

How many times did my siblings and I look up at our loving mother and ask, "When's dinner? When can I go outside and play? When will Dad be home?"

Mom often smiled and gave the response mothers have offered since the beginning of time: "Patience is a virtue." Maybe. But I wonder—what if we've all been wrong? What if patience isn't just a moral virtue? Perhaps patience is an *active* word, a verb to *live,* not an attribute to *live by.*

If so, there might be eternal value in learning to be anxiously engaged *and* patient at the same time. For me to sit on the curb and quietly wait for the dinner bell or for Dad to pull into the driveway was good. But chasing one more butterfly, pulling weeds for Mom, or reading a good book might have been even better.

Because we're imperfect, it's fair to say we've all struggled with patience at some point in our journey. In fact, I'm *still* asking the questions. "When will the home repair be done? When will my child call me back? When will the Utah Jazz win an NBA title?"

Whether you're a basketball fan or not, can you imagine patiently waiting for your team to win the most coveted trophy in sports—a championship? We're patient and prudent, of course, but we don't sit around quietly waiting for our turn. We're *actively* patient; we've turned patience into a verb. Because to be *impatient* could mean becoming foolish, imprudent, and impulsive. The only way to win a championship is to consistently work, plan, prepare, and tackle each day with patience for a better tomorrow.

In the spring of 2017 I had knee surgery, and it might have been nice to hang around the bedroom and heal. I certainly had to be patient with my body, but I healed though active waiting. I went through rehabilitation. I pushed myself.

In that case, patience wasn't just a verb, it was a painful one. Today I'm back at full strength, all because I was actively waiting through the healing process. Patience isn't just waiting, and just waiting isn't patience. Every good result requires action.

It's a lifelong pattern. How I loved to watch my children grow! They were at the mercy of parents—or older siblings—for every need. They waited to have their diaper changed, or to be fed, or to go to bed. But they rarely sat quietly and waited. They continued to explore, to test, and to learn.

PATIENCE ISN'T JUST WAITING, AND JUST WAITING ISN'T PATIENCE. EVERY GOOD RESULT REQUIRES ACTION.

As teenagers, they needed patience to blossom from awkward into attractive and from shy into outgoing. Teens can't rush crossing the threshold from childhood into adulthood, but they also can't sit and wait and simply cross their fingers and hope it happens.

When I think of moments of impatience in my life, they are often tied to a weakened relationship with the Savior. During my late teens, when I began to drift from the influence of the Church and my parents, I found myself increasingly selfish and self-absorbed. I stopped cultivating uplifting friendships and raced the calendar to become an adult.

Larry was similar, and we found ourselves living as if there were just the two of us in our own little world. We didn't make time for friends; we spent nearly every waking minute together. Though we were still kids in many ways, we thought we were self-sufficient and shouldn't have to answer to anyone.

After our wedding, we were ready to tackle the world. Larry was playing softball, and back then he had to attend church once a month so he could be eligible to play on the Church team. Still, we were too selfish to socialize, and we got to know only teammates and not many other members of the ward.

I remember one man who was assigned to be our home teacher. He wanted to get to know us, which I appreciate now, but I sure didn't back then. One Sunday morning he showed up and knocked on the door, and there we were—in our pajamas. I opened the door, thinking, "I don't want to deal with you. Don't try to make me come to church. I'm not ready. I don't want that. I'm busy. I'm having a good Sunday."

I didn't say all that aloud, but I was impatient and rude. I asked him to leave us alone and told him he didn't have any right to visit on a Sunday morning. I shut the door and immediately recognized my mistake. Still, my pride kept me from opening it up again to apologize. Instead, I walked away from my side of the door and he walked away from his.

What a shameful memory. My relationship with the Lord and His gospel wasn't where it should have been, and I had become impatient with one of His servants. That good man had probably made a goal to be a perfect home teacher and to deliver a message of love from the Lord and the ward. Maybe all he wanted was to share a brief prayer with my small family. I don't know where he is today, but if I could find him, I'd gladly open my door and exercise the kind of patience I didn't possess back then.

When our friends have trials we can't fix, when our kids struggle, when our spouses are diagnosed with illnesses, we might pray and demand instant responses. I know I have. But there's an important relationship between patience and prayer.

As impatient children of a perfect Father in Heaven, we sometimes forget that answers come on God's schedule, not ours. So we pray, we ask, and while we wait, we should live life. We learn

> AS IMPATIENT CHILDREN OF A PERFECT FATHER IN HEAVEN, WE SOMETIMES FORGET THAT ANSWERS COME ON GOD'S SCHEDULE, NOT OURS.

and grow. We don't stay on our knees all day patiently waiting. After the praying, we wait patiently on our feet, in motion and always seeking to do good. I pray daily to know how to better lead the company that bears my last name. But then, after a period of pondering, I have to get up, stretch myself, and make decisions.

———

A journalist once asked me, "Gail, what has been your biggest trial or test of your patience?"

I smiled and said, "Larry." Then I quickly amended my answer. "But he was also my biggest blessing." Life with Larry gave me ample opportunities to learn and practice patience. Sometimes it felt like I was pulling on the reins of a runaway horse, and it was all I could do to regain control of my life. At other times it seemed like I was galloping as fast as I could, but I couldn't get anyone to move forward with me.

I knew I would need to become friends with patience when, after six years of dating and courtship, Larry still didn't think it had been quite long enough. He was a visionary man, but in practical terms he couldn't always imagine his future, and so marriage was not on his radar. That required me to take matters into my own hands. So, I decided to practice some active waiting by being the one to propose.

After we had been married for several years, we found ourselves in debt for the first and only time. Instead of growing discouraged, we went to work. We patiently solved the problem, but we sure didn't wait around while doing it.

Unfortunately, this created a different kind of stress—Larry was always working. My husband soon started putting in endless hours, and it seemed like we never had time with each other. I tried to be patient and endure this unexpected life, but I knew I needed to become more active in solving the problem. I had to be creative to find ways for us to spend time together.

One evening I decided to pack up the kids and take them to work to see Larry. We went to a nearby restaurant and had a great time. So we did it again, then again, and developed a pattern of eating together a couple of times a week. It wasn't easy, but it worked. I learned to live patience by fixing a problem where I had control to do so.

As much as I love my new husband, Kim, and I know he loves me, blending two lives at our ages requires patience. Like any couple who marries a second time, or perhaps later in life, there are compromises to be made, habits to adjust, and countless opportunities to blend preferences. It takes patience, but not waiting.

We talk, we serve one another, we give in here and there

on minor things so the things that really *do* matter—harmony, trust, unity, and love—can grow. In any healthy marriage, the more we live patience as a verb, the closer we feel to heaven.

Like any mother, I've had to live patience at a hundred miles per hour with my children, too. I love my kids dearly, but I'm not embarrassed to say they each stretched my patience muscles in different ways. When they were younger, I wondered if I could mold them into who I thought they should be. But over the years of learning and becoming a better mother, I realized I didn't need to change them; I needed to accept them for who they were—children of God with individual talents.

> I LOVE MY KIDS DEARLY, BUT I'M NOT EMBARRASSED TO SAY THEY EACH STRETCHED MY PATIENCE MUSCLES IN DIFFERENT WAYS.

I lived with faith that they would come through their difficult times, and I loved them in spite of their occasional desires to test their schoolteachers, Church leaders, and me. I learned patience not by waiting but by actively praying, loving, and serving. My children aren't perfect, and I'm sure I've been an imperfect mother, but they're incredibly good, honest, and loving people in a world that doesn't always reward those attributes. No matter what direction they go in this life or the next, I will be patient and loyal with them until the end of eternity.

If you've lost a loved one, particularly after a long illness, you know a lot about turning patience into an active word that's always in motion. During Larry's battle with diabetes, there were many times when patience was the only thing that could get us through the day. Once he was out of the hospital, it seemed like every day was an endless round of doctor visits, treatments, physical therapy, shots, and making sure correct medications were given in the correct doses, all while trying to meet each other's emotional needs and struggling to maintain a household.

Because of my eternal perspective and understanding that this life is but a moment and then all things will be made whole, I could endure what I was going through and try to help Larry to endure his struggles too. I was able to exercise active patience because it was important for me to be able to know I had done everything I could to make life good for him without having any regrets. I'm filled with peace and contentment about our life together, especially during the challenges of his final months.

I remember vividly the day Larry asked a good friend from church who was visiting his bedside during a particularly difficult time, "What is it I am supposed to be learning from this? This is so hard."

The friend answered, "I'm not sure it's anything you have to learn; it's what you are teaching others."

If I could have finished that sentence, I would have added, " . . . teaching others about patience."

———

Whenever I speak to groups of women who feel like they can never catch up, as if a balanced life were always just beyond reach, I remind them they belong to the largest club of women on earth. Every mother has wondered if bedtime will ever arrive, if her husband will be home for dinner, or if she will ever successfully juggle kids, work, church and those online college classes. These are the days that truly test our patience.

Whether we're a mom, a wife, a CEO, or all of the above, we've had those moments. We desperately want to be so much more, and we're impatient about getting there. But if my journey has taught me anything, it's to love myself and the life I have. I know that because of God's grace, we're all doing better than we think we are.

The Lord knows it takes active patience and courage to be His disciples, and losing our patience over our husbands, children, Church callings, or clients doesn't make us any less worthy of discipleship.

I've often reminded myself when my patience is tested that all adversity has a purpose. If we believe Christ is perfect—and I do—then my trials are meant for me. They're a custom challenge designed by Someone who doesn't just love me, He wants me to pass the test. We can't become like Him if we don't experience patience-trying adversity. If it was important for His ministry, it should be for ours, too.

Like all principles, patience isn't something that stands alone. When we link it with courage and turn them both into verbs, we can overcome any obstacle at our own speed.

I'm grateful for the days I've struggled with patience. I've become stronger and more knowledgeable. When I wonder if my patience is down to the last speck, I think about how much my Savior has done for me and how He never, ever runs out of patience.

I don't intend to run out of patience for Him, either.

Success Is Relative

Writing Your Own Definition

Just before Larry died, our youngest son had a special conversation with his father. Bryan loved and admired his dad and aspired to be just like him. He said, "Dad, it will be my honor to live my life trying to be like you and measuring myself against you."

Larry looked at him intently and said, "Son, don't measure yourself against me. Measure yourself against yourself. It is enough."

Larry's counsel remains profound. There's a risk in measuring ourselves against others, whether they are parents, mentors, or other heroes. We are each unique in our own way. I agree with his sound advice; if I could add my own twist, I would suggest we measure ourselves against the standard and the potential God has for us. Just as Jesus Christ sought to do the Father's will, so can we, and in doing so, we become like Him.

This is a good place to start a discussion on success and, ultimately, to end it. It might be tempting to look at those around us and impatiently see their shortcomings or to focus exclusively on our own: Why didn't I finish college when I had the chance? Why can't I manage to keep my car in good repair? Why does my neighbor struggle to keep a steady job? Why doesn't that woman do her visiting teaching? Doesn't she know how much she has to offer?

It's crucial to understand the difference between how the world measures success and how it's measured in heaven. To me, real success has at least three components:

1. The depth of our relationship with God.
2. The quality of our relationships with others.
3. Our stewardship over the gifts and resources God has entrusted to us.

Once when I was chatting with a friend who homeschools her children, she lamented that she had not finished college, the house wasn't always clean at bedtime, and her schedule made it tough to fulfill her Church calling. She felt those things were a reflection of her, and to some extent that might be true. On the other hand, she's married to a good man, and they keep their covenants. They're raising sons who honor the priesthood, daughters who have their eyes fixed on the temple, children who each desire to make the world a better place. To me, that kind of success is much more important than being a CEO of a billion-dollar company. These are eternal successes—the kind that endure.

I'm not saying that worldly successes aren't important; they are. We mostly measure ourselves by our daily efforts. So, if all our efforts are based on eternal principles, they will have a stronger foundation and deeper rewards.

> IT'S CRUCIAL TO UNDERSTAND THE DIFFERENCE BETWEEN HOW THE WORLD MEASURES SUCCESS AND HOW IT'S MEASURED IN HEAVEN.

This viewpoint might be controversial in today's world, and maybe I'm old-fashioned in my thinking, but I believe that whenever possible, it's good to have one parent working and one in the home when raising children. I know that's not always possible, obviously, and my company employs more than 11,000 men and women, many of whom have spouses who also work outside the home, but one of our goals is to provide quality jobs that promote this value. President David O.

McKay's famous declaration remains true: "No other success can compensate for failure in the home."

Each morning when I plan my day, I find that there is usually more to accomplish than there are hours available. I try to prioritize from the most urgent items to the things that could wait if I can't get to them that day. Then I give my time over to the Lord. He always sees the big picture and, with His guidance and my work, we usually get the right combination of things done. It's always interesting to me to watch how He rearranges things as the day progresses. My job is to stay in tune and be flexible.

At night, I kneel by my bed and ask in prayer if I have done all that He expected of me that day. If I can feel a reassuring "yes" or something even close to a "yes," I consider myself successful. Our Creator only asks us to do our best with what we're given.

It's important to recognize that success for you might look different than success for your neighbor. If you feel the need to compare yourself to someone, look up and compare yourself against the measure God has set for you.

As a youngster, I learned how hard life can be by watching my parents try to provide for a large family when resources were scarce. I remember watching my father work hard every day. He never had a regular job in an office with the security of knowing that tomorrow's paycheck was guaranteed, but he tried diligently to find work and support our family. Though he was never wealthy or even terribly comfortable, his definition of success was obvious to me. He loved his wife and family, used all his energy to raise good children, provided the necessities for his family, and honored his priesthood covenants. His life was hard; he had many challenges and health issues and would not likely be recognized by anyone but his family for having done anything remarkable. He passed away at fifty-six, far too young, but I will always think of him as a successful man because his successes were eternal. His treasures were laid up in heaven.

Each of us has to decide how we will choose our success. I have some friends who have struggled for many years to keep their home and pay their bills while raising a family and being faithful to their callings in the Church. They lived in a middle- to upper-class neighborhood and were determined to stay there even though they couldn't afford it. Outsiders who wanted to judge them might have said they were being foolish to try to maintain their "status quo." The husband was highly educated but had trouble holding down a job. The wife was intent on staying at home with the children rather than taking a job outside the home. Without knowing all the facts and circumstances, it would have been easy to judge them, but not

> WE WILL NEVER ESCAPE TRIALS, BUT MAKING DECISIONS WITH AN EYE TOWARD HEAVEN IS ALWAYS A GOOD CHOICE.

very wise. We must always be mindful of the difference between worldly success and eternal success. It's possible that they did exactly what they felt the Lord wanted them to do and were willing to learn whatever was needed while going through this test. We will never escape trials, but making decisions with an eye toward heaven is always a good choice.

Having a look at independence through my own eyes gave me a chance to define success while spreading my wings. When I worked as a telephone operator, I occasionally dealt with irate customers who thought I should be able to find anything in seconds. They wanted me to be their "Google" before there was even an Internet. I took this as a personal challenge.

If I could keep that kind of customer happy, then I'd done my job in a way that pleased me and my boss. It made me feel successful, and each time it happened I felt more confident. I took pride in being able to help a customer who was ranting and raving because another operator couldn't spell a difficult name or didn't have any desire to go beyond the basic question, "Do you know the spelling?"

For me to feel successful, I needed to push a bit harder. "Let's keep looking. Is there another way to spell it? Could it be this? Let's look under that." When I found the listing, I felt so satisfied. I hadn't saved someone's life, hit the winning basket, or closed a big business deal, but I'd been perfectly successful in that specific situation. We can all do at least one thing perfectly. When we create opportunities for change, when we challenge ourselves in what we might call self-competitions, we can feel the success of growth. Are you better today than you were yesterday? That's success.

Sadly, the world wants us to believe that being successful is exclusively about material things. It's how much money you make or which office you're in or what kind of car you drive. For those who stay home, success is judged by whether your kids are perfectly dressed on Sundays, or your meals look like they were cooked by a professional chef, or your Instagram account overflows with photos of perfect vacations. To me, perfect teeth and perfect fashion aren't success, just marketing.

Success can be the simple satisfaction of doing something well, and it's important to remember that the definition changes based on where we are in life. A mother who gets her two toddlers and a baby to and from Target without losing her mind—or a child—should feel like a *huge* success. Years later,

SUCCESS CAN BE THE SIMPLE SATISFACTION OF DOING SOMETHING WELL, AND IT'S IMPORTANT TO REMEMBER THAT THE DEFINITION CHANGES BASED ON WHERE WE ARE IN LIFE.

when those children are teenagers and can be more helpful, she might expect much more.

Imagine that same young mother has another child already in elementary school and the teacher is pressing her to become active in the PTA or to be a classroom volunteer or to serve as a field-trip chaperone. It's probably too much, and if this tender mother says "yes" to anything more than she can handle, she could be setting herself up to feel like a failure. But if she keeps her eyes fixed squarely on the here and now, and on what makes for a successful day as *she* defines it, she'll feel the peace of mind and confirming influence of the Spirit that she's right on track with the Lord's will. When I see that mom juggling groceries and managing tantrums in the checkout line, I want to hug her and say, "You're doing just fine! This *is* success! You're an amazing mother."

At some point those kids will grow up and become more independent, and the time will be right for volunteering in the classroom, tagging along on the field trip, or running for

PTA president. Then she can write a new definition of success for that chapter of her life.

After my children were grown and married, I was asked to serve on the board of trustees at Salt Lake Community College. I thought, "Ah, there's a whole new world here. This is an area that I've never been able to take on before because I've been fulfilling my wife and mother role." But now, with this opportunity to jump into civic engagement, I felt another kind of fulfillment.

Some success comes through serving, growing, and developing talents that we didn't even know we had. I was able to learn what it takes for students to apply and complete their college education, and I was able to shake their hands at graduation. I reviewed college policies and procedures, gave talks to students, and conducted meetings as the chair of the board of trustees. If I had tried to take that on when I was younger and had children at home, even teenagers, I wouldn't have been successful with either one.

Success wears many outfits. When our oldest son, Greg, was five months old, he rolled off our bed and suffered a serious subdural hematoma. Two surgeries were needed to remove the blood clots on his brain; thankfully, both were successful.

But at the time, I sure didn't feel like a successful mom. I had not protected my child from being seriously injured. With a lot of prayers and priesthood blessings he recovered fully, and I'm eternally grateful for that blessing.

Thankfully, Larry and I had insurance that paid for most of the medical bills. But when all was settled, we were several thousand dollars in debt for the first time in our marriage. We decided that we needed to get out of debt as soon as possible, so we sat down and listed our expenses on a piece of paper from the lowest bill to the greatest and added a payoff date for each. We continued to make the payments on each of our bills monthly, and as the one with the shortest time frame was paid, we put that extra money toward the next bill, and so on as each bill reached the end of its term. It took time, but we felt a new kind of success as we watched the balances shrink.

> GOING WITHOUT MIGHT BE A BETTER MEASURE OF SUCCESS THAN HAVING IT ALL.

Then one day, a customer at Larry's work brought in a beat-up Land Cruiser as a trade-in on a new car. Larry was able to buy it for $800, fix it up, and sell it for $2500. The profit paid off our remaining debt, and suddenly we were back in the black. From that day on, we never went into personal debt again, and I consider that more of a success than the money we've been blessed with. It's not easy, but being consumer debt-free in today's quick-loan world is a definition of success worth striving for. It's hard, I know. But it's interesting that going without might be a better measure of success than having it all.

Back then, we didn't buy anything we didn't need. I remember we didn't often buy birthday gifts for extended family because we couldn't afford them. A card was all we could manage. The first year we were married, I gave our original wedding pictures as gifts at Christmas because we couldn't afford to buy anything for our parents. We'd made priorities, and although there wasn't much under our tree or the trees of our loved ones that Christmas, we felt successful because we were in control of our finances.

Larry used to say the public perception was that everything he touched turned to gold. But people rarely heard the rest of the story. In reality, he and I had plenty of failures. Those things are not as interesting, I suppose, but our perceived success has become a trap for some people who examine our lives from a distance. Everyone has failures; it's part of the plan.

I would say that from the beginning, honesty is what made us successful. We were real. We didn't have to put on a show for employees, bankers, or investors. We insisted on authenticity and we felt good about ourselves. Not that we'd been perfect, but that we'd been perfectly ourselves. That's the first kind of success, because if you're not successful within your own mind, it's hard to be successful anyplace else. You can be humble and meek and still say to yourself, "I'm doing pretty well, you know? I'm valuable. I have confidence."

I've always laughed that people thought we were somehow different after we bought the Utah Jazz. I'll never forget a reporter coming to do an interview with me shortly after that purchase. I met him at the door wearing a pair of sweatpants with a small pinhole in the leg and a white shirt. I suppose he thought it was strange that I hadn't dressed up for the interview. He actually included that in his story. Then, a few days after we purchased the team, I was in a store buying fabric for drapes for my mother's house. I knew the saleslady well, and she introduced me to another customer who'd been watching me. The first thing out of her mouth was, "You don't look like somebody who has eight million dollars."

I was stunned. "We don't," I said. "The bank's got it."

I think it's natural for people to be curious about public figures, but I've never worried about what people think of me. The truth is, the dealerships, the Jazz, the movie theaters, none of those things define success. You and I are successful when we align our will with God's, whether the public knows our name or not.

It's obvious that in sports, the ultimate measure of success is a championship, and no one wanted to win an NBA title as much as Larry H. Miller. But time and time again, even after the close losses to the Chicago Bulls, Larry and I remained committed to our values. We continue to look for players of good character who reflect what we stand for. We hire good coaches who know how much the team means to our community. We can and will use our resources to enrich lives with good, wholesome entertainment, and as we do, we will continue to enjoy strong support from our fans and add economic value to our communities.

When he was still playing competitive softball, Larry lamented how often other teams bent the rules to write their own twisted definition of success. Larry's teams were nationally ranked and often competed for championships. But when faced with the chance to look the other way or condone a deal that was against league rules, he refused. He wanted to win a championship the right way. When they failed to bring home the trophy, they started all over again the next year feeling no less successful. Disappointed, yes. Dishonored, no.

The same is true for the Jazz. We understand that each team starts on equal footing in October and by June there is only one champion. Let's not sugarcoat it, we want that trophy in Utah as much as anybody. That's what we play for. We put the best team we can on the floor and hope that *this* is the year. But if our players play their very best, if we entertain our fans and treat everyone well, we can deliver a successful experience. When we win a title, and we will, we'll do it the right way! Good guys don't always finish last.

———

Earlier in our marriage, when the company really began to fire on all cylinders and we began to have additional opportunities for growth, Larry said something I'll never forget: "I think we're being prepared for something, but I don't know what it is." Nothing ever clearly manifest itself, so we filed that thought away and kept moving forward.

Several years later Larry raised it again. "I think Heavenly Father is preparing us to be stewards over the resources He has provided for us because He knows He can trust us to do good with them. He is putting us in a position to do His will. He has trusted us with a special stewardship, and we should do as much good as we're able. We need to look at life that way."

Larry and I both believed that if we fulfilled that purpose, we'd be successful, and it wouldn't matter what kind of car we drove or where we lived. The Lord expected us to bless others in whatever way we could. Money became a tool to do good things with.

In June of 2008, Larry had a heart attack as a complication of his diabetes. A year and a half before that, he had called our children and me together around the kitchen table and handed us notebooks, telling us that we would want to take notes. We met together every week for the following year and a half for the express purpose of learning everything we needed to know to run the company when he was ready to slow down and turn the business over to the kids. Although he had diabetes, he was managing it and was planning to live for a long time. In February of 2009, he passed away.

Despite the preparation, when Larry died, I still thought, "Can this company survive without him? What about all these employees and their families?" I wondered if that prompting Larry had might have died with him.

Thankfully, it didn't. I determined that my new role would include preserving and growing the legacy we started in 1979 with our first dealership even though I had never worked in the company. The company hasn't just continued to grow since Larry's passing, it's grown faster than ever. Our children have stepped up and continued to add to our success. Our employees have embraced our family's vision and values. I understand that Heavenly Father still has work for us

HEAVENLY FATHER STILL HAS WORK FOR US TO DO TO FULFILL THE MEASURE OF OUR STEWARDSHIP AND CONTINUE TO "GO ABOUT DOING GOOD UNTIL THERE IS TOO MUCH GOOD IN THE WORLD," AS LARRY OFTEN SAID.

to do to fulfill the measure of our stewardship and continue to "go about doing good until there is too much good in the world," as Larry often said.

When I'm asked to speak on success, I sometimes trot out a list of accomplishments that sound impressive from the stage. I don't share them to boast, but to bolster the point of my unexpected journey.

I reveal that I still go to the office almost every day and oversee one of the two hundred largest privately owned businesses in the country, which also happens to be the tenth-largest privately owned auto group. We do business in forty-seven states and I'm the president of more than eighty companies. I was recently nominated to represent Utah at the national competition as the Time Magazine Dealer of the Year. Along with Larry, we were named Entrepreneurs of the Decade by Mountain West Capital Network. I was dubbed Utah's most influential person in sports. I serve on the board of Intermountain Health

Care. I have three honorary doctorate degrees. Until recently I served as the chair of the board of trustees of Salt Lake Community College and I'm a member of the President's Leadership Council at BYU. I serve on the National Advisory Council at the University of Utah. I have a Silver Beaver award from the Boy Scouts of America. Oh, and I have the final say on who plays for the Utah Jazz if I want to exercise it.

Impressive, I suppose, but only if those things are what the Lord wants for me at this stage of my life. If the Lord suddenly asked for something else, if He asked me to give it all up and follow another path, I'd like to think I would have the faith to do it.

President Gordon B. Hinckley once shared this advice with students at Brigham Young University: "You are good. But it is not enough just to be good. You must be good for something. You must contribute good to the world. The world must be a better place for your presence. And the good that is in you must be spread to others." I like that advice, and I think following it will guarantee success.

When I give commencement speeches, I share similar counsel. I invite grads to be resourceful, to use their talents, and then to develop even more. I promise that God will help them if they help themselves. I plead with them to do something that makes them happy and to be prepared when opportunity comes their way. But I also warn them that failure is coming and not to fear it. They can always start over, and they'll be stronger each time they do. I also like to teach that the real recipe for success is investing in yourself and others. Give back. Pay it forward.

The more I think about my success, the more I cling to the lessons I learned in the home of my youth. I've been poor and I've been rich, but none of that really matters because I'm the same person either way. I'm an imperfect daughter of God trying to do what He thinks is best for me and never forgetting that life isn't about one huge achievement—it's a series of successful moments strung together by little victories at home, work, and church and in the community.

And probably a lot of courageous trips to Target.

Your Voice

Find It, Use It

Believe it or not, for many years I didn't have the courage to say my own name. When someone extended a hand I would shake it, but if I said anything at all, I'd offer, "I'm Larry's wife."

One night in the mid-eighties, just after we'd bought the Jazz, we were waiting together in a line for food at a nice reception. Someone came over to speak to Larry and literally did not look at me even once. It was as if I'd waited in the car.

Later that night, as we readied for bed, I said, "Larry, you're growing in ways I cannot even understand. The experiences you are having are changing you. How am I going to keep up or get to your level? I don't want to be left behind."

I was living in a shadow that grew every single day. Gail Miller was just a stay-at-home mom with no education, but Larry H. Miller was becoming the man who saved the Jazz, the man with his name on the dealerships, the man with the movie theatres, the restaurants, the baseball team, and so on. I was just an appendage with no value to add other than giving an opinion no one ever heard but him.

I began to notice how rarely I referred to myself. When I spoke outside the home, it was usually about Larry's life, Larry's interests, and Larry's successes. I don't think anyone ever noticed that I wasn't even identifying myself. I was essentially a nameless woman with observations on a famous man. On bad days, I felt like another fan or customer at one of the dealerships that bore his name.

At times it was even worse. Not only did I not have courage to say my own name, but I felt completely invisible. Every time we stood in a line or walked into a room, people recognized Larry. I didn't mind that, of course, and he loved engaging with people. He was gracious and treated everyone kindly. But as these exchanges took place, I seemed to disappear. I was a nobody, or at least I felt that way.

One day while I was visiting a counselor for help with one of my children, the doctor looked across at me and said, "I'm happy to help your child, but you're the one who really needs my help."

In my heart, I knew he was right. I began receiving professional counseling, and I would have to say those years of counseling saved me, my marriage, and a lot more. In my first session, I learned so much about what was missing in my inner core. I had lost my voice and my confidence. It was time to find them again.

In our early sessions, I started to feel myself reconstituted as a woman and daughter of God. I learned to say my name and claim my identity. I discovered how often I was subjugating my opinion in subtle but damaging ways. One exercise involved having me recognizing the difference between two simple phrases. When I usually said, "Isn't that a pretty tree?" the counselor instructed me to say, "*I* think that's a pretty tree." It's a subtle difference, but it gave me a voice.

I learned to make statements that reflected my own thoughts, ideas, and creativity. He taught me I have a right to respectfully say, "This is who I am, and this is who I want to be." Slowly I became a person again, with an identity that was my own and wasn't dependent on my husband or my kids. The sessions weren't some magic spell that made all my insecurities vanish. Those changes took time and a lot of work. But with every

I LEARNED TO SAY MY NAME AND CLAIM MY IDENTITY. I DISCOVERED HOW OFTEN I WAS SUBJUGATING MY OPINION IN SUBTLE BUT DAMAGING WAYS.

trip I came home feeling both a little lighter about my burdens and a little stronger about my will.

Eventually I realized that to save my marriage, I needed Larry to join me. It might not be the right approach for every couple, but I gave my husband an ultimatum. Either he joined me in counseling, or we needed to give serious consideration to whether we could even work together for the sake of the marriage and the family. To Larry's great credit, he came. It wasn't easy, but he recognized we needed help. I thank heaven he did.

Side by side we uncovered our ability to exercise our right to be individuals and be equally yoked at the same time. We learned how to work to prepare to meet Heavenly Father again. What kind of marriage did we want to present? I learned so much about Larry during our sessions, and he learned a lot about me. We had unique voices and could each bring something to the choir.

Our rides to and from counseling were as valuable as the sessions themselves. I got to see the man Larry was becoming, and he got to see the real woman he'd married. I was in awe of what he knew, of his ability to discern trends and patterns, of his charisma. He was in awe of how much I'd learned about the business just by sitting on the floor next to him while he soaked in that yellow bathtub. And he learned to value me as his wife and the mother of our children.

Every chance I get, and it's not often enough, I beg anyone who will listen to get counseling if the thought has crossed his or her mind for even a moment. If you've ever wondered whether you need it, you do. It's not easy, and far too many people give up after the first tense session or burst of contention, but if you stick with it, the results are almost universally positive.

Remember that when we break an arm, we seek medical attention. When we have heart troubles, we seek medical attention. It shouldn't be any different when we're depressed, anxious, or living in a marriage that needs help. There isn't shame in getting help, but there might be in pretending we don't need it.

> IF YOU PUT YOUR RELATIONSHIP FIRST AND TEND TO IT PROPERLY, LIKE ANY OTHER LIVING THING, IT WILL GROW.

Husbands and wives must recognize that as leaders of the family, they're affecting everyone downstream. It's not just about the marriage, it's about Mom and Dad. If you put your relationship first and tend to it properly, like any other living thing, it will grow. If you don't, it will wither and may die.

When I've gone back in my mind to periods of my life when my voice was louder and more courageous, I have seen that it was when I took time for myself. I pursued my own hobbies and talents. I was happiest playing sports and moving outside my comfort zone. It's hard to find out what your voice sounds like if you're not using it.

Though the world provided my education (I didn't go to college), I decided later in life to take a writing class at the University of Utah. I didn't take it because I was looking for a job or some great door to open, I just wanted to learn how to express myself in my writings. I knew that writing would be another way to use my voice.

Maybe you can make your voice heard through painting, or songwriting, or leading a company or a team or a school. Maybe you'll use your actual voice to sing in ways that inspire and invite the Spirit. Has it been too long since you've used whatever voice is in you?

My mother found her voice by going back to school at age sixty-one to become a nurse. She was forty years older than most of the other students on graduation day. Until she could no longer handle the rigors of the job because of age, she worked in labor and delivery. I was so proud of her desire to keep learning, stretching herself, and blessing others all her life.

After Larry died, I knew I would need my voice more than ever to ensure a smooth transition of the company. As part of planning for succession, I enrolled my children and myself in a special course at Harvard University that focused on family businesses. We learned so much together and I left there more confident than ever.

Speaking of confidence, I worry that too many women have had some of the same negative experiences I've had. I've found that women in the Church are terribly hard on themselves, perhaps more so than any other group. We feel guilty when we're late for stake conference, or when dinner isn't ready when the missionaries arrive, or when we forget to send a birthday card, or when we don't raise our hand to make a meal for a sister whose husband died.

As partners in the priesthood, we have a different kind of strength than anyone else in the world, and we shouldn't be shy about it. Women have an ability to make a difference in the world in a way that men don't. Maybe we're afraid of making a mistake, or not being accepted, or not having the right voice at the right time, but I know that if we can overcome that fear, we can see and feel that we're endowed with certain qualities that can bless every person in our circle of influence.

When we use our voice of kindness, compassion, knowledge, and forgiveness, we can link with the Lord to change hearts.

It's time to stand up with courage. We cannot shy away from our responsibilities or opportunities to testify of Christ in the way we live. Standing tall doesn't just benefit us, it also blesses the world that watches. And trust me, the world is indeed watching. We have divine talents and a mandate to use them! Not sure yet where yours might be hiding? That's okay. Pick up a pencil, or sit at a piano or a sewing machine or in an MBA executive course or at a canvas. Then ask Heavenly Father for help. He's listening.

Have faith in yourself. You can make a difference—in fact, you already have. And don't worry if at the end of your journey you haven't cured a disease, or solved a community crisis, or written a hit song. There's a 100 percent chance that if you've loved well, served often, and used your voice for good in whatever way you could, you've impacted at least one other child of God. What a legacy!

No one is lost. I truly believe there's always hope, that we

> IT'S TIME TO STAND UP WITH COURAGE. WE CANNOT SHY AWAY FROM OUR RESPONSIBILITIES OR OPPORTUNITIES TO TESTIFY OF CHRIST IN THE WAY WE LIVE.

can change, that we can find the light and live a better life. Yes, it's hard work and it's not automatic. We can't just wish for it; we have to make it happen.

It's true, my life has been an unexpected journey. But I bet yours has been too. Isn't that part of the joy? My trials have not been any more difficult than yours. They've just been mine, prepared for me by a loving Heavenly Father who knew exactly what trials and blessings I would need in order to grow. There is still a lot I don't know, but I have no doubt that He knows precisely how to help me, Gail Miller, find the courage to be me.

My friend, I guarantee that if you listen, He also knows just how to help you find the courage to be you.

Notes

Page ix: "Gratitude unlocks the fullness . . ." Melody Beattie, accessed online at https://www.values.com/inspirational-quotes/7164-gratitude-unlocks-the-fullness-of-life-it.

Page 34: "I teach them correct principles . . ." Joseph Smith, as quoted in John Taylor, "The Organization of the Church," *Millennial Star,* November 15, 1851, 339.

Page 52: "There is no limit to what a man can do . . ." Quotation from plaque in Oval Office, Ronald Reagan Presidential Foundation and Institute.

Page 87: "I have to live with myself, and so . . ." "Myself," Edgar A. Guest, Collected Verse of Edgar A. Guest (Cutchogue, NY: Buccaneer Books,1976).

Page 88: "Make new friends, but keep the old . . ." Joseph Parry, "New Friends and Old Friends," in *The Best-Loved Poems of the American People* (New York: Doubleday, 1936).

Page 134: "No other success . . ." David O. McKay, quoting

J. E. McCulloch, *Home: The Savior of Civilization* (Southern Co-operative League: 1924), 42.
Page 147: "You are good. . . ." Gordon B. Hinckley, "Stand Up for Truth," Brigham Young University Devotional, September 17, 1996.